Research
Briefings
1987

Research
Briefings
1987

for the Office of Science and Technology Policy,
the National Science Foundation,
and Selected Federal Departments and Agencies

Committee on Science, Engineering,
and Public Policy
National Academy of Sciences
National Academy of Engineering
Institute of Medicine

NATIONAL ACADEMY PRESS
Washington, D.C.   1988

National Academy Press   2101 Constitution Avenue, NW   Washington, DC 20418

The National Academy of Sciences (NAS) is a private, self-perpetuating society of distinguished scholars in scientific and engineering research, dedicated to the furtherance of science and technology and their use for the general welfare. Under the authority of its congressional charter of 1863, the Academy has a working mandate that calls upon it to advise the federal government on scientific and technical matters. The Academy carries out this mandate primarily through the National Research Council, which it jointly administers with the National Academy of Engineering and the Institute of Medicine. Dr. Frank Press is President of the NAS.

The National Academy of Engineering (NAE) was established in 1964, under the charter of the NAS, as a parallel organization of distinguished engineers, autonomous in its administration and in the selection of members, sharing with the NAS its responsibilities for advising the federal government. Dr. Robert M. White is President of the NAE.

The Institute of Medicine (IOM) was chartered in 1970 by the NAS to enlist distinguished members of appropriate professions in the examination of policy matters pertaining to the health sciences and health of the public. In this, the Institute acts under both the Academy's 1863 congressional charter responsibility to be an adviser to the federal government and its own initiative in identifying issues of medical care, research, and education. Dr. Samuel O. Thier is President of the IOM.

The Committee on Science, Engineering, and Public Policy is a joint committee of the National Academy of Sciences, the National Academy of Engineering, and the Institute of Medicine. It includes members of the councils of all three bodies.

This work was supported by the National Science Foundation under Grant LPA8501382.

Library of Congress Catalog Card Number 87-63132

International Standard Book Number 0-309-03828-6

Printed in the United States of America

Committee on Science, Engineering, and Public Policy

KENNETH J. RYAN, Kate Macy Ladd
Professor of Obstetrics and Gynecology,
Harvard Medical School, and Chairman,
Department of Obstetrics and
Gynecology, Brigham and Women's
Hospital, Boston, Mass.
*LEON T. SILVER, William M. Keck
Foundation Professor of Geology,
Division of Geological and Planetary
Sciences, California Institute of
Technology, Pasadena
HERBERT A. SIMON, Richard King Mellon
University Professor, Department of
Computer Science and Psychology,
Carnegie-Mellon University, Pittsburgh,
Pa.

*Term expired June 30, 1987

Ex Officio

FRANK PRESS, President, National
Academy of Sciences
ROBERT M. WHITE, President, National
Academy of Engineering
SAMUEL O. THIER, President, Institute of
Medicine

COSEPUP Staff

ALLAN R. HOFFMAN, Executive Director
MYRON F. UMAN, Associate Executive
Director
BARBARA A. CANDLAND,
Administrative Coordinator
CATHY D. DYSON, Senior Secretary

RESEARCH BRIEFING TOPICS

Topics cited below are followed by the names of units that provided staff support for their development. A collected volume is published each year as *Research Briefings 1987*, *Research Briefings 1986*, etc., by the National Academy Press, Washington, D.C.

1987

1. Order, Chaos, and Patterns: Aspects of Nonlinearity (*Commission on Physical Sciences, Mathematics, and Resources*)
2. Biological Control in Managed Ecosystems (*Commission on Life Sciences*)
3. Chemical Processing of Materials and Devices for Information Storage and Handling (*Commission on Physical Sciences, Mathematics, and Resources*)
4. High-Temperature Superconductivity (*Committee on Science, Engineering, and Public Policy*)

1986

1. Science of Interfaces and Thin Films (*Commission on Physical Sciences, Mathematics, and Resources*)
2. Decision Making and Problem Solving (*Commission on Behavioral and Social Sciences and Education*)
3. Protein Structure and Biological Function (*Institute of Medicine*)
4. Prevention and Treatment of Viral Diseases (*Institute of Medicine*)

1985

1. Remote Sensing of the Earth (*Commission on Physical Sciences, Mathematics, and Resources*)
2. Pain and Pain Management (*Institute of Medicine*)
3. Biotechnology in Agriculture (*Board on Agriculture*)
4. Weather Prediction Technologies (*Commission on Physical Sciences, Mathematics, and Resources*)
5. Ceramics and Ceramic Composites (*Commission on Engineering and Technical Systems*)
6. Scientific Frontiers and the Superconducting Super Collider (*Commission on Physical Sciences, Mathematics, and Resources*)
7. Computer Vision and Pattern Recognition (*Commission on Physical Sciences, Mathematics, and Resources*)

1984

1. Computer Architecture (*Commission on Engineering and Technical Systems*)
2. Information Technology in Precollege Education (*National Academy of Sciences*)
3. Chemical and Process Engineering for Biotechnology (*Commission on Physical Sciences, Mathematics, and Resources*)
4. High-Performance Polymer Composites (*Commission on Physical Sciences, Mathematics, and Resources*)
5. Biology of Oncogenes (*Institute of Medicine*)
6. Interactions Between Blood and Blood Vessels (Including the Biology of Atherosclerosis) (*Institute of Medicine*)
7. Biology of Parasitism (*Institute of Medicine*)
8. Solar-Terrestrial Plasma Physics (*Commission on Physical Sciences, Mathematics, and Resources*)
9. Selected Opportunities in Physics (*Commission on Physical Sciences, Mathematics, and Resources*)

1983

1. Selected Opportunities in Chemistry (*Commission on Physical Sciences, Mathematics, and Resources*)

2. Cognitive Science and Artificial Intelligence (*Commission on Behavioral and Social Sciences and Education*)
3. Immunology (*Institute of Medicine*)
4. Solid Earth Sciences (*Commission on Physical Sciences, Mathematics, and Resources*)
5. Computers in Design and Manufacturing (*Commission on Engineering and Technical Systems*)

1982

1. Mathematics (*Commission on Physical Sciences, Mathematics, and Resources*)

2. Atmospheric Sciences (*Commission on Physical Sciences, Mathematics, and Resources*)
3. Astronomy and Astrophysics (*Commission on Physical Sciences, Mathematics, and Resources*)
4. Agricultural Research (*Board on Agriculture*)
5. Neuroscience (*Institute of Medicine*)
6. Materials Science (*Commission on Engineering and Technical Systems*)
7. Human Health Effects of Hazardous Chemical Exposures (*Commission on Life Sciences*)

Preface

Research Briefings 1987 is the sixth volume of research briefing reports published by the Committee on Science, Engineering, and Public Policy (COSEPUP).* It brings to 36 the number of such reports prepared on a broad range of topics since the first volume in 1982 (see the list of topics on page vii). The briefings are prepared at the request of the President's Science Advisor, who also serves as Director of the Office of Science and Technology Policy (OSTP), and the Director of the National Science Foundation (NSF).

The four reports in this collection are on the topics High-Temperature Superconductivity; Chemical Processing of Materials and Devices for Information Storage and Handling; Order, Chaos, and Patterns: Aspects of Nonlinearity; and Biological Control in Managed Ecosystems. The superconductivity briefing was prepared at the specific request of the NSF director after the 1987 briefing activity was under way, in response to the exciting new developments in superconductivity in ceramic oxide materials announced early in 1987.

*COSEPUP is a joint committee of the National Academy of Sciences (NAS), the National Academy of Engineering (NAE), and the Institute of Medicine (IOM).

Research briefing topics generally are selected by the OSTP and NSF directors in the late fall in response to suggestions put forward by COSEPUP. COSEPUP's suggestions are selected from a much larger list of suggestions offered by the commissions and boards of the National Research Council (NRC); members of the NAS, NAE, and IOM Councils; members of COSEPUP; as well as officials of the NSF and the OSTP. Individual briefings are designed to assess the status of a field and identify high-leverage research opportunities and barriers to progress in the field (including where appropriate, progress in commercial exploitation). They also assess U.S. capabilities in the field vis-à-vis those in other nations. The briefings are then prepared by panels of experts, usually in the spring, with the day-to-day assistance of NRC staff. This schedule allows time for COSEPUP review in late spring and presentation of the briefings, in both oral and written form, to federal officials early in the upcoming fiscal year's budget preparation cycle. The briefing reports, both in individual form and as an annual collection, are then published by the National Academy Press.

Over the years the value of these relatively

brief but comprehensive overviews of various frontier fields of science and technology has been recognized more broadly. The information provided by the research briefings proved to be of value not only to government officials responsible for R&D planning and budget preparation, but also to officials of industry and to university personnel responsible for setting research priorities. Foreign science and technology officials have also shown strong interest in the research briefing reports. Most of the credit must go to the volunteer experts who serve on the panels, and to the NRC units and staff who so ably support the panels' day-to-day activities. I also want to acknowledge the confidence and continued support of the OSTP and the NSF for the research briefing activity, as well as the efforts of my colleagues on COSEPUP who serve so effectively as reviewers of the reports. It is only through the efforts of all these individuals and groups that preparation of the reports is possible.

Gilbert S. Omenn, *Chairman*
Committee on Science, Engineering, and Public Policy

Contents

Report of the
Research Briefing Panel on
High-Temperature Superconductivity

Research Briefing Panel on High-Temperature Superconductivity

John K. Hulm (*Chairman*), Director, Corporate Research and R&D Planning, Westinghouse R&D Center, Pittsburgh, Pa.

Neil W. Ashcroft, Professor of Physics, Cornell University

Roger W. Boom, Professor and Director, Applied Superconductivity Center, Nuclear Engineering and Metallurgical Engineering, College of Engineering, University of Wisconsin, Madison

H. Kent Bowen, Ford Professor of Engineering, Massachusetts Institute of Technology

Robert J. Cava, Technical Staff, AT&T Bell Laboratories, Murray Hill, N.J.

Paul C.W. Chu, Temple Chair in Science, University of Houston, Tex.

John Clarke, Professor of Physics, University of California, Berkeley, and Principal Investigator, Lawrence Berkeley Laboratory

Marvin L. Cohen, Professor of Physics, University of California, Berkeley

James S. Edmonds, Senior Project Manager, EPRI, Palo Alto

Douglas K. Finnemore, Associate Director, Science and Technology Division, Ames Laboratory, Department of Energy

Eric B. Forsyth, Chairman, Accelerator Development Department, Brookhaven National Laboratory

Theodore H. Geballe, Professor of Applied Physics, Stanford University

David C. Larbalestier, Associate Director, Applied Superconductivity Center, Department of Metallurgical Engineering, University of Wisconsin, Madison

Charles Laverick, Private Consultant, Patchogue, N.Y.

Alexis P. Malozemoff, Division Coordinator for High-Temperature Superconductivity, T.J.Watson Research Center, IBM Corporation

James H. Parker, Private Consultant, Penn Hills, Pa.

David Pines, Professor, Loomis Laboratory of Physics, University of Illinois, Urbana

Carl H. Rosner, President, Intermagnetics General Corporation, Guilderland, N.Y.

John Rowell, Assistant Vice President, Solid State Science and Technology Research Laboratory, Bell Communications Research, Red Bank, N.J.

Arthur Sleight, Research Leader, Central Research and Development Department, Experimental Station, E.I. duPont de Nemours & Company

James L. Smith, Senior Scientific Advisor, Center for Materials Science, Los Alamos National Laboratory

Masaki Suenaga, Senior Metallurgist, Department of Applied Sciences, Brookhaven National Laboratory

Maury Tigner, Director, SSC Central Design Group, Universities Research Association

Michael Tinkham, Rumford Professor of Physics and Gordon McKay Professor of Applied Physics, Harvard University

John Williams, Head, Magnet Technology Division, National Magnet Laboratory, Massachusetts Institute of Technology

Committee on Science, Engineering, and Public Policy Staff

Allan R. Hoffman, *Executive Director*

John R. B. Clement, *Staff Officer*

Barbara A. Candland, *Administrative Coordinator*

Cathy D. Dyson, *Senior Secretary*

Nisha Govindani, *Senior Secretary*

Report of the
Research Briefing Panel on
High-Temperature Superconductivity

EXECUTIVE SUMMARY

The recent discovery of superconductivity at temperatures up to 95 K is one of the more important scientific events of the past decade. The sheer surprise of this discovery, as well as its potential scientific and commercial importance, largely underlie the degree of excitement in the field. Because our previous understanding of superconductivity has been so fundamentally challenged, a door has been opened to the possibility of superconductivity at temperatures at or above room temperature. Such a development would represent a truly significant breakthrough, with implications for widespread application in modern society.

While the base of experimental knowledge on the new superconductors is growing rapidly, there is as yet no generally accepted theoretical explanation of their behavior. Applications presently being considered are largely extrapolations of technology already under investigation for lower-temperature superconductors. To create a larger scope of applications, inventions that use the new materials will be required. The fabrication and processing challenges presented by the new materials suggest that the period of pre-commercial exploration for other applications will probably extend for a decade or more.

Near-term prospects for applications of high-temperature superconducting materials include magnetic shielding, the voltage standard, superconducting quantum interference devices, infrared sensors, microwave devices, and analog signal processing. Longer-term prospects include large-scale applications such as microwave cavities; power transmission lines; and superconducting magnets in generators, energy storage devices, particle accelerators, rotating machinery, medical imaging systems, levitated vehicles, and magnetic separators. In electronics, long-term prospects include computer applications with semiconducting-superconducting hybrids, Josephson devices, or novel transistor-like superconducting devices.

The United States has a good competitive position in the science of this field, and U.S. researchers have contributed significantly to the worldwide expansion of scientific knowledge of the new materials. International competition is intense. Several other leading industrialized countries have mounted substantial scientific and technological efforts, especially Japan, a number of Western European nations, and the USSR.

The short-term problems and long-term potential of high-temperature superconductivity may both be easily underestimated. Given this potential and the current limited understanding of the new superconducting materials and their properties, it is essential that government, academic institutions, and industry take a long-term, multidisciplinary view. Since science and technology in this field are strongly intertwined, progress must occur simultaneously in basic science, manufacturing/processing science, and engineering applications. It is also important to maintain an open and cooperative international posture.

The panel has identified eight major scientific and technological objectives for a national program to exploit high-temperature superconductivity. They are:

1. to improve understanding of the essential properties of current high-temperature superconducting materials (especially T_c, H_{c2}, J_c, and alternating current losses) through the acquisition of additional experimental data;

2. to develop an understanding of the basic mechanisms responsible for superconductivity in the new materials;

3. to search for additional materials exhibiting superconductivity at higher temperatures by the synthesis of new compositions, structures, and phases;

4. to prepare thin films of controllable and reproducible quality from present high-temperature superconducting materials and to establish preferred techniques for growing films suitable for electronic device fabrication;

5. to develop bulk conductors from current high-temperature superconducting materials, with special emphasis on enhanced electric current-carrying capacity;

6. to advance the understanding of the chemistry, chemical engineering, and ceramic properties of the new materials, focus-ing on synthesis, processing, stability, and methods for large-scale production;

7. to fabricate a range of prototype circuits and electronic devices based on superconducting microcircuits or hybrid superconductor/semiconductor circuits, as suitable thin film technologies become available; and

8. to fabricate a range of prototype high-field magnets, alternating and direct current power devices, rotating machines, transmission circuits, and energy storage devices, as suitable bulk conductors are developed.

The panel recommends that the following actions be taken to carry out the objectives listed above:

• The U.S. government should proceed with its plans to provide funding for high-temperature superconductivity research and development on the order of $100 million for fiscal year 1988. This funding level represents a good beginning in addressing the challenges and opportunities offered by the new materials.

• Sufficient new money must be provided both to the science and the technology of high-temperature superconductivity so that other important and promising areas of research and development are not held back.

• A mechanism should be established to monitor the potential demand for increased scientific and technical manpower if the promise of high-temperature superconductivity is fully realized, and to make appropriate recommendations on the funding of U.S. graduate and postgraduate research programs.

• An interagency mechanism should be established to help coordinate planning for superconductivity programs among the various federal agencies.

• Given the anticipated rate of advance in high-temperature superconducting science and technology, the federal government should review progress in the field after 12 months as a guide to future resource allocation.

• Through its agencies, the U.S. government must enhance the probability that U.S. industry gains a competitive advantage in this new field. This could be accomplished by the close association of industry with the Engineering Research or Science and Technology Center programs of the National Science Foundation, by cost-sharing between government and industry on proof-of-concept projects, and by other joint efforts.

• An important mechanism for enhancing U.S. industry's position is improved technology transfer from the national laboratories to the private sector. Although a variety of means are already in place to encourage such transfer, the panel is concerned about the effectiveness of past efforts and urges both government and industry to pursue linkages more aggressively.

INTRODUCTION

Perhaps the most remarkable feature of the discovery of high-temperature superconductivity is the fact that it was so unexpected. The sheer surprise of this discovery, as well as its potential scientific and commercial importance, largely underlie the degree of excitement and fervor of the field. Superconductivity in the past has always been a challenging fundamental and technological problem, for which understanding and application have come slowly. Because our previous understanding of superconductivity has been so fundamentally challenged, there is hope that the progress that has been achieved so dramatically in the past 18 months can be continued.

High-temperature superconductivity offers an important opportunity for our nation's scientific and technological community. The opportunity merits a substantial thrust in fundamental research; at the same time, enough is already known to encourage commercial development efforts with the newly discovered materials.

BACKGROUND

Superconductivity was discovered by a Dutch scientist, Kamerlingh Onnes, in 1911. He found that the electrical resistance of frozen mercury (Hg) disappeared suddenly at 4.2 degrees Kelvin (K) (-269 degrees Celsius [C]), a temperature accessible only through immersion in liquid helium. In 1913 Onnes also found that weak magnetic fields (of a few hundred gauss) destroyed the effect, with the metal reverting to its normally resistive state. Subsequently, other metals such as tin (Sn) and lead (Pb) were found to be superconductors at similarly low temperatures. People soon began to invent applications for superconductors—for example, to reduce losses in electric power systems. However, in the 1920s it was found that superconductivity disappeared in these metals when rather low electric currents were passed through them. As a result, power applications were abandoned.[*]

Significant progress in understanding the physical basis of superconductivity came in the 1950s. In the theory of Bardeen, Cooper, and Schrieffer, interaction between electrons and "phonons" (vibrational modes in the lattice of atoms making up the material) leads to a pairing of electrons. At low temperatures, these so-called Cooper pairs condense into an electrical superfluid, with energy levels a discrete amount *below* those of normal electron states (known as the superconducting energy gap). In the same period, new materials were discovered that displayed superconductivity at temperatures as high as 20 K, almost 5 times higher than the temperature of superconductivity in mercury.

These scientific discoveries had two important consequences. First, in a direct experiment to verify the energy gap, Giaever at the General Electric Research Laboratories observed electron tunneling between superconductors—that is, electrons passing from one superconductor to another through a thin insulating barrier. The observation of normal electron tunneling led Josephson in England to speculate that Cooper pairs could also tunnel through a barrier, a prediction that was soon verified by Rowell and Anderson at Bell Laboratories. These discoveries laid the foundation for a whole new superconducting electronics technology.

Second, Kunzler and coworkers at Bell Laboratories established that a group of superconducting compounds and alloys (the Type-2 superconductors) could carry extremely high electric currents (up to a million amperes per cm^2 of conductor cross-section) and remain superconducting in intense magnetic fields (up to 30 tesla [T] or 300,000

---

[*]Electric utility equipment typically carries thousands of amperes and has associated magnetic fields of up to 20,000 gauss or 2 tesla.

gauss). These materials, offering the prospect of very high magnetic fields and current-carrying capacity at a much lower cost than before, revived interest in superconducting magnets and electric power components.

In the years between 1960 and 1986, several hundred materials were found to be superconducting at sufficiently low temperatures. However, the highest critical temperature (i.e., the temperature below which a material becomes superconducting, T_c) achieved in this period was 23 K, which still required either liquid helium or liquid hydrogen cooling.

The workhorse of the high-field magnet technology has been niobium-titanium (NbTi), a ductile alloy that can be made into wires. A second material of great promise, niobium-tin (Nb_3Sn), can support even larger electric currents and remain superconducting in higher magnetic fields, but it has found much less use because of its brittle nature. Other materials have found more limited uses—for example, pure niobium in radiofrequency cavities and niobium nitride (NbN) in electronics.

RECENT DISCOVERIES

Recently, new materials have been discovered that have substantially higher T_cs. In January 1986 Bednorz and Müller, working at the IBM Laboratory in Zurich and searching for superconductivity in previously unexplored materials, determined that a lanthanum-barium-copper ceramic oxide became superconducting at temperatures over 30 K.

Spurred on by this unexpected discovery, laboratories in the United States and elsewhere have since found materials with even higher T_cs. The highest stable value to date that has been independently confirmed, 95 K (-178 C), was first achieved by Chu and colleagues at the University of Houston working with Wu and coworkers at the University of Alabama. At this temperature, liquid nitrogen (which boils at 77 K at atmospheric pressure and is much cheaper than liquid helium) can be used for cooling.

A large number of the so-called high-temperature superconductors are now known to exist, all of them variations of two basic types (the so-called 40 K and the 95 K [or 1-2-3] materials). Those with T_c greater than 77 K are based on only one structure, with copper (Cu) and oxygen (O) a constant feature. The new materials present an enormous scientific opportunity and open new vistas for potential applications. Because our understanding of superconductivity has been challenged in so fundamental a fashion, with the present theoretical understanding of superconductivity being insufficient to explain the properties of the new materials, there is hope that what has been achieved in such a short time can be extended. The excitement surrounding the field has caught the imagination of policymakers, the media, and the public at large. Research students are also attracted by this excitement, often being drawn from other areas of science by the prospect of careers in the field; but it is important to note that they are drawn from a manpower pool that can only be expanded slowly. *

There have been several preliminary reports of superconductivity at still higher temperatures, but at present there is no consensus as to their validity. It is likely that room-temperature superconductivity would make possible a much broader range of applications. A more immediate concern is whether the present high-temperature superconductors can be used to improve present electronic or power applications; on this question, researchers worldwide are cautiously optimistic.

*Some of the manpower issues are discussed in *Physics Through the 1990s: An Overview*, Washington, D.C.: National Academy Press, 1986.

CURRENT KNOWLEDGE OF THE NEW HIGH-TEMPERATURE SUPERCONDUCTORS

The new high-temperature superconductors are mixed metal oxides that display the mechanical and physical properties of ceramics. A key to the behavior of the new materials appears to be the presence of planes containing copper and oxygen atoms chemically bonded to each other. The special nature of the copper-oxygen chemical bonding gives rise to materials that conduct electricity well in some directions, in contrast to the majority of ceramics, which are electrically insulating.

The first class of high-T_c oxides discovered was based on the chemical alteration of the insulating ternary compound La_2CuO_4 by replacement of a small fraction of the element lanthanum (La) with one of the alkaline earths barium (Ba), strontium (Sr), or calcium (Ca). The substitution led to compounds with critical temperatures of up to 40 K. In these materials, an intimate relation between superconductivity and magnetic order is presently under intensive study and has inspired one of the many classes of theories that attempt to explain high-temperature superconductivity.

In a second class of compounds, based on $YBa_2Cu_3O_x$ (where Y is yttrium, a rare earth), the metallic atoms occur in fixed proportions. These are the so-called 1-2-3 compounds, which are highly sensitive to oxygen content, changing from semiconducting, at $YBa_2Cu_3O_{6.5}$, to superconducting near 95 K at $YBa_2Cu_3O_7$, without losing their crystalline integrity. The high sensitivity of their properties to oxygen content is due to the apparent ease with which oxygen can move in and out of the molecular lattice.

The 40 K and 1-2-3 (or 95 K) materials have similar structures but differ significantly in other respects. In both compounds, the rare earth and alkaline earth atoms provide a structural framework within which the chains of copper and oxygen atoms may be hung.

Surprisingly, the substitution of other rare earths, even magnetic ones, for yttrium in the 95 K compounds results in very little change in superconducting properties. Various substitutions are under study, both to understand the present materials and to achieve higher critical temperatures in new ones.

STATUS OF THEORETICAL UNDERSTANDING

In the microscopic theory of Bardeen-Cooper-Schrieffer, the presence of a net attractive interaction between conduction electrons, which would normally repel each other because of their like electrical charges, is essential to the occurrence of superconductivity. In conventional superconductors this attraction originates in the dynamic motion of the crystal lattice, which leads to an attractive "electron-phonon-electron" interaction. But the recent appearance of superconductivity in a class of materials quite different from the conventional superconductors, and with extremely high transition temperatures as well, has led physicists to explore a very wide spectrum of possible new pairing mechanisms involving, for example, spin fluctuations, acoustic plasmons, and excitonic processes. The physical origin of the pairing "glue" remains an open and to some extent crucial question. There is a wide range of theoretical possibilities, and the ultimate explanation may involve a combination of mechanisms. Indeed, some theorists have discarded conventional Bardeen-Cooper-Schrieffer theory and have suggested that there may not even be the traditional close relationship between energy gaps and basic superconducting properties.

Given the wealth of puzzling experimental features in a variety of different materials, it may take a considerable effort, with a diverse theoretical program, to unravel fully the secrets of these compounds. In the meantime the fact that they obviously do exist can form the basis of immediate commercial exploitation. But the prospect of even more promising materials has led to a substantial theoretical effort aimed at elucidating the principles underlying the phenomenon. Typical of the questions currently under active consideration are the role played by oxygen, the nature and scope of dynamic mechanisms and the resulting electron pairing, whether this coupling is weak or strong, and whether the anisotropic nature of the materials is a truly important feature. The appearance of superconducting coherence lengths 1 or 2 orders of magnitude smaller than those previously encountered, the very low carrier concentrations, and the apparent importance of both copper and oxygen will probably require a considerable extension of our current understanding of superconductivity. The fact that the superconducting interaction mechanism in the new materials is likely to be very different from that in low-temperature superconductors certainly enhances the prospect that other high-temperature superconducting materials may be discovered.

PHYSICAL PROPERTIES IMPORTANT FOR TECHNOLOGY

The most important physical properties for applications are the superconducting critical temperature (T_c), the upper critical magnetic field (H_{c2}), and the maximum current-carrying capacity in the superconducting state (J_c). Also important are the mechanical, chemical, and electromagnetic properties: physical and thermal stability, resistance to radiation, and alternating-current loss characteristics. Each is discussed more fully below.

Critical Temperature, T_c

A rule of thumb for general applications is that materials must be operated at a temperature of ¾ T_c or below. At about ¾ T_c critical fields have reached roughly half their low-temperature limit, and critical current densities roughly a quarter of their limit. Thus, to operate at liquid nitrogen temperature (77 K), one would like T_c near 100 K, making the 95 K material just sufficient. To operate at room temperature (293 K) one requires a material with T_c greater than 400 K, well above the highest demonstrated value. Higher T_c materials would be superior across the board for applications, other properties being acceptable, and materials with T_cs above 400 K would have a truly revolutionary impact on technology. In this temperature domain one could consider mass market applications.

Upper Critical Magnetic Field, H_{c2}

$YBa_2Cu_3O_7$ samples generally exhibit extremely high upper critical fields. Preliminary measurements indicate that for single crystals H_{c2} is anisotropic, that is, dependent upon field direction relative to the *a-*, *b-*, or *c*-axes of the orthorhombic lattice. Values ranging from 30 T (*c*-axis) to 150 T (*a-* or *b*-axes) are reported at 4.2 K. The mechanical stresses associated with the confinement of such high magnetic fields in typical compact geometries are frequently beyond the yield or crushing strengths of known materials. Hence, improving these intrinsic H_{c2} values is less important than increasing T_c or J_c values. In fact, materials with higher T_cs should exhibit higher H_{c2} values if the performance of known materials is any guide. However, developing materials that can practically be fabricated into magnets and that retain useful J_cs at fields approaching H_{c2} even at 77 K is an important challenge.

Critical Current Density, J_c

For practical applications, J_c values in excess of 10^3 amperes per square millimeter (A/mm^2), are desirable both in bulk conductors for power applications and in thin film superconductors for microelectronics.

Bulk ceramic conductors of $YBa_2Cu_3O_7$ have achieved about 10^2 A/mm^2 at 4.2 K and 6 T. However, J_c falls off very steeply to levels around 1–10 A/mm^2 at 77 K and 6 T. These J_c values are determined from magnetization measurements; J_c values derived from transport measurements are usually lower. There is no clear understanding of these reduced J_c levels at the present time, but achieving acceptable values for J_c in bulk high-temperature superconductors is of critical importance and must be a principal focus of research on fabrication processes.

Based on current experience, a reasonable target specification for a commercial magnet conductor would be J_c of 10^3 A/mm^2 at 77 K and 5 T, measured at an effective conductor resistivity of less than 10^{-14} ohm-m,* with strain tolerance of 0.5 percent, and availability at prices comparable to or less than those of conventional low-temperature superconductors.

Preliminary measurements on epitaxially grown single-crystal thin films indicate J_c values in excess of 10^4 A/mm^2 at 77 K and zero magnetic field. These values seem adequate for microelectronic applications.

Mechanical Properties

Present ceramic high-temperature superconducting materials can be strong, but they are always brittle. Hence, it may be that high-temperature superconductors wire will be wound into magnets prior to the final high-temperature oxidation step in its fabrication, after which it becomes very brittle. Other conductor fabrication techniques might be feasible, however—for example, those used for producing flexible tapes of Nb_3Sn. An elastic strain tolerance of 0.5 percent may be achieved in a multifilamentary conductor by a fine filament size and by induced compressive stresses.

*The sensitivity of many of the measurements reported on the new ceramics is poor, and "zero resistance" often means 10^{-10} to 10^{-7} ohm-m, 4 to 7 orders of magnitude greater than values required for practical application.

Currently available ceramic technology allows the fabrication of the kinds of complicated pieces that may be needed for such applications as radiofrequency cavities. There are some indications that the new materials may be deformable above 800 C and can then be shaped. The development of a mechanical forming process, however, is constrained by the parallel need for the process to optimize J_cs, both by aligning anisotropic crystal grains and by increasing the strength of the intergranular electrical coupling.

Life testing will also be necessary to understand the performance of materials under realistic conditions such as temperature cycling and induced stresses due to transient fields. The adhesion of high-temperature superconductors to other materials is important in microelectronics, in which temperature cycling results in thermal expansion and contraction that cause stresses at the interface. More attention is needed to this problem.

Chemical Stability

The 1-2-3 compounds readily react with the ambient atmosphere at typical ambient temperatures. These problems seem to be less severe, however, as the purity and density of the materials are improved. Both water and carbon dioxide participate in the degradation through the formation of hydroxides and carbonates. Further study of the nature of this degradation is needed to develop handling procedures or protective coatings that will ensure against impairment of superconducting properties by atmospheric attack.

Chemical stability is also limited because oxygen leaves the structure under vacuum, even at room temperature. Surface protection techniques need to be developed to allow satisfactory performance and lifetime of the materials under various conditions of storage and operation. These concerns are heightened in thin films, in which, for some applications, the chemical composition of the outer atomic layers near the surface must be maintained through many processing steps, and in which diffusion into the substrate interface could degrade superconducting properties.

Radiation Effects

High-temperature superconductors appear to be somewhat more sensitive to radiation than conventional superconductors. High sensitivity to radiation damage could pose a difficult, although not insurmountable, problem for application to magnetic fusion machines. For electronic applications the substitution of either conventional or high-temperature superconducting devices for those employing semiconductors would result in an improvement of several orders of magnitude in resistance to radiation damage.

Alternating Current Losses

Conventional superconductors exhibit losses in alternating current applications, such as in 60 Hertz power transmission or in microwave devices. Although little is known about the alternating current characteristics of the new high-temperature superconductors, there is no reason to expect that the new materials will exhibit lower alternating current losses than other superconducting materials. Recent measurements on thin films in parallel applied fields show the presence of a large surface barrier for the entry of flux, which indicates that hysteresis losses would be small. More extensive measurements of such losses are required.

SYNTHESIS AND FABRICATION

Two steps are required to synthesize the 95 K superconducting materials. First, the basic structure must be formed at temperatures above 600–700 C. The tetragonal structure so formed is deficient in oxygen and does not possess superconducting proper-

ties. Accordingly, the second part of the synthesis involves annealing under oxygen at a temperature below 500 C. The arrangement of this additional oxygen in the lattice causes a conversion from tetragonal to orthorhombic symmetry that supports high-temperature superconductivity.

For the future development of high-temperature superconducting materials, we require a much better understanding of how synthesis conditions relate to the structure of the 1-2-3 compounds on the atomic and nanometer scales. We need to know, further, how this structure relates to superconducting properties and to other important properties such as chemical stability and mechanical strength.

The fabrication of many high-temperature superconducting ceramics involves grinding of prereacted starting materials, which can result in contamination from grinding media. At the present time there is no evidence that impurities introduced by grinding degrade superconducting properties; however, further work is required to optimize this process. Also, the rate of oxygen uptake during the oxygen anneal depends on the available surface area of the sample; for large particles or very dense ceramics, this critical oxygen uptake reaction can be slow. A recently announced fabrication technique, in which materials in bulk are made by melting the ingredients, may make the manufacture of wires and specially shaped pieces much easier and may eliminate the need to work with sintered materials.

In addition, processes are required for the commercial production of high-quality thin films on useful substrates. What is needed is to compare the various ways that have been used to produce thin films—electron beam, planar magnetron sputtering, pulsed laser evaporation, molecular chemical vapor deposition—and establish the strengths and weaknesses of each method. Epitaxial growth methods also need to be studied.

A further requirement is the achievement of reliable, low-resistance ohmic contacts to the new materials. A better understanding of phase equilibria, solid solutions, and intermetallic compounds is needed to find stable ohmic contacts that do not degrade superconducting behavior.

NEW SUPERCONDUCTING MATERIALS

Finally, we must not neglect the search for new compounds with intrinsically superior superconducting properties. Operation at 77 K leaves little margin when running a device that utilizes a superconductor with a T_c of 95 K. Cryogenic systems that operate below 77 K should be investigated, and the compatibility of high-temperature superconductors with refrigerants other than liquid nitrogen (e.g., liquid neon) should be tested. Further, and perhaps most importantly, the events of the past year have shown that surprises do occur, and it may be that superconductivity at or above room temperature may be detected at some future date in compounds not yet studied.

CURRENT FIELDS OF APPLICATION AND THE LIKELY IMPACT OF THE NEW MATERIALS

Virtually all of the applications currently envisioned for high-temperature superconductors are extrapolations of devices already operated at liquid helium temperatures. The most important applications, however, may well involve devices that have yet to be contemplated, much less invented.

As shown in Table 1, present and potential applications fall into several distinct classes. Present applications include high-field magnets, radiofrequency devices, and electronics. Superconductivity brings unique advantages to high-field applications because resistive conductors such as copper dissipate large amounts of energy as heat when carrying large currents. Superconductors are also useful in high-Q cavities because of their low alternating current losses at high frequencies compared to those in normal metals.

TABLE 1 Principal Applications of Superconductivity[a]

PRESENT APPLICATIONS
  Magnets
  • Commercial and industrial uses
    —Medical diagnostics and research (magnetic-resonance imaging and spectroscopy)
    —Radiofrequency devices (gyrotrons)
    —Ore refining
    —R&D magnets
    —Magnetic shielding
  • Physics machines (colliders, fusion machines, radiofrequency cavities)
  Electronics
  • Sensitive accurate instrumentation (superconducting quantum interference devices, infrared sensors)
  • Electromagnetic shielding

POTENTIAL APPLICATIONS
(Proven superconducting technology, but no current market adoption)
  • Power utility applications
    —Energy production (magnetohydrodynamics, magnetic fusion)
    —Large turbogenerators
    —Energy storage
    —Electrical power transmission
  • Transportation
    —High-speed trains (magnetic levitation)
    —Ship drive systems
  • Computers
    —Semiconducting-superconducting hybrids
    —Active superconducting elements

[a]There are many other potential applications, some of which are mentioned in the text.

Electronic applications for superconductors usually involve low electric currents (although high current densities) and low magnetic fields. The core element has been a unique bistable device, the Josephson junction. Superconductors may also eliminate resistive current losses in electronic lines and device interconnections. In addition, various kinds of superconducting sensors have been produced. All of these applications, including the assembly of superconducting electronic components into larger devices, will be reconsidered with the new compounds.

Potential applications of high-temperature superconductors divide into those relevant to currently available materials with critical temperatures near 95 K, and those relevant to possible future materials with higher critical temperatures. The most exciting possibilities, of course, arise with materials with critical temperatures above room temperature.

HIGH-FIELD AND LARGE-SCALE APPLICATIONS

Superconducting magnets using liquid helium technology have been successfully applied for a number of years in engineered systems and development projects in hospitals, mines, industrial plants, laboratories, and transportation systems. Most of these applications require multiple technologies, with superconductivity playing a critical role.

In medicine, superconductors have been a significant factor in the development of a new market. In high-energy physics, superconductors have led to machines of unprecedented and previously inconceivable energy. In electric power, potential applications in energy storage and power transmission equipment promise to extend the capacity and range of current technology. Superconducting magnets are essential components in experimental systems for magnetic fusion and magnetohydrodynamics (MHD). The extremely high power-to-weight ratio possible for superconducting machines makes them particularly attractive for space applications.

For magnet and power applications, the higher the critical temperature, the smaller will be the scale at which commercial viability will be achieved. As an example, the power level at which motors and generators become competitive will be much lower than

with the present low-temperature superconductors, when compared to nonsuperconducting machines. A liquid nitrogen-cooled motor, for instance, operating at modest current and magnetic field, might well be smaller, more efficient, and more reliable for the same power output than many present-day motors.

For most applications the switch from liquid helium to liquid nitrogen technology is not revolutionary but will lead to improvements. The continued need for refrigeration is a disadvantage and will reduce market penetration. Of course, the reconsideration of applications held to be impractical at liquid helium temperatures might lead to new products. A hollow conductor cooled with liquid nitrogen is easy to visualize in practical use, for instance. It may not be necessary to demand that the technical specifications of new materials compete with the best commercial superconducting materials of today: a conductor of modest specifications may have value in a wider context than conventional low-temperature superconductors. The new materials, in short, may not so much replace present-day superconductors as extend the applications of superconductivity to a larger circle of users.

Medical Applications

Magnetic-resonance imaging (MRI) and spectroscopy (MRS) constitute radically new techniques in medical diagnosis and treatment, and their full impact is yet to be realized. Much more widespread availability of MRI and MRS systems can be anticipated, with concomitant reductions in cost and enhancement of features. The use of high-temperature superconducting materials would likely bring further small reductions in the costs of manufacture and operation. The redesign of MRI and MRS systems with liquid nitrogen cooling would also make them more user-friendly and reliable by reducing cooling system complexity.

Superconducting Radiofrequency Cavities

If microwave alternating current loss characteristics are tolerable, the new superconductors may greatly improve the performance of superconducting radiofrequency cavities by allowing them to operate at higher fields. Indeed, the potential impacts embrace all of microwave power technology, especially in the promising millimeter-wave region. Accelerator technology might also be significantly advanced by the availability of liquid nitrogen-cooled superconducting cavities. The applicability of superconducting technology to recirculating linear accelerators, on the other hand, is an accepted fact. In addition to providing high-quality beams for nuclear physics research, these machines are natural candidates for continuous beam injectors used in free-electron lasers. As technology matures and industrial applications develop for high-power, high-efficiency tuneable lasers in biotechnology, fusion plasma heating, and other fields, superconducting radiofrequency devices will proliferate.

Transportation

Ambitious attempts to apply superconductivity to land and ocean transportation have been made over the years with some success in the United States, Europe, and Japan. In fact, a Japanese magnetic levitation rail system is available for interested buyers and is economically viable.

Superconducting ship propulsion systems were studied in England in the 1960s. The U.S. Navy successfully installed a prototype superconducting drive system on a small ship in 1980; the development of a 40,000-horsepower drive system continues. A second concept uses seawater as the working fluid in an MHD propulsion system; the drive scheme is known as an electromagnetic thruster (EMT). Ship models based on this propulsion principle were promoted in the United States in the 1960s and operated in Japan in the 1970s. Practical designs for a full-scale EMT ship have been proposed, and industrial collaboration is being sought.

Because the present worldwide systems of air, sea, and land transportation are well established and represent a substantial investment, society has not yet made use of the potential advantages that have been demonstrated in prototype transportation systems using low-temperature superconductors. In land-based systems the principal advantage is high speed. Ship-based systems are lighter, have better speed control, and permit the radical rearrangement of power drive systems within ship structures. The combination of room-temperature superconductors and the low specific volume of superconducting machines could revolutionize surface transportation.

ELECTRONIC APPLICATIONS

Some of the most promising applications of high-temperature superconductors are electronic systems involving thin film lines or Josephson elements. Applications in computers would have the largest commercial impact, but may take longer because of their complexity. Sensor and instrument applications are simpler and are likely to be commercialized within a few years. Simplest of all is the use of high-temperature superconductors for low-field electromagnetic shielding.

Computers and Logic Devices

Much work has already been carried out on computer subsystems based on liquid helium superconductors. Semiconductor technology is still advancing rapidly, however, and continues to dominate the computer field. The discovery of high-temperature superconductors may change this situation.

One possible role of superconductors in such systems is simply to interconnect the semiconducting devices with superconducting microcircuit transmission lines. This possibility is already interesting at 77 K, because certain semiconducting devices switch faster at this lower temperature. However, 77 K copper lines present significant competition because of their decreased resistivity compared to that at room temperature.

The most exciting opportunities would use room temperature superconductors, offering compatibility with the entire line of semiconductors, including the highest performance bipolar devices. In the most promising scenario, the use of room temperature superconductors could affect the full range of data processing systems, which form the largest high-technology industry in the world today.

Although the implications of high-temperature superconductors for semiconducting computer systems have yet to be assessed, the reduced losses compared to normal conductors offer many possible advantages. System performance (i.e., switching speed) can be increased by reducing the RC time constant associated with the interconnect line. Narrower lines can be used, saving space on the chip. The elimination of power losses and voltage drops permits miniaturization of power busses and potentially, therefore, of the entire system.

The high-temperature superconductors have also been proposed for computer applications using Josephson junctions. High-temperature superconductors may offer higher device switching speeds, higher bandwidth transmission, and the possibility of using semiconducting memory to supplement ultra-high-speed superconducting logic. The disadvantages of high-temperature superconductors are increased thermal noise and switching power losses at 77 K compared to earlier liquid-helium temperature designs.

A variety of superconducting transistor-like devices have been proposed, among them superconducting field-effect transistors (FETs), several nonequilibrium devices, and optically switched FETs. These devices are at early stages of development, even using the conventional low-temperature superconductors; but although there are still considerable materials and fabrication problems, the potential performance of some of these devices might be enhanced by higher switching speeds and output voltage changes stemming from the larger energy gaps of the high-temperature superconductors.

SENSORS AND OTHER APPLICATIONS

SQUIDs

Superconducting quantum interference devices (SQUIDs), operating at liquid helium temperatures as sensitive magnetic field detectors, are already of value in many disciplines including medical diagnostics, geophysical prospecting, undersea communications, and submarine detection. SQUIDs made with the new high-temperature materials have been operated at liquid nitrogen temperatures. Relatively inexpensive SQUID-based magnetometers operating at 77 K or higher would be deployed in large numbers if electrical noise can be held to acceptably low levels.

Radiation Detectors

Superconducting microwave and far-infrared radiation detectors (quasiparticle mixers, superconducting bolometers) already exist using conventional superconductors. In spite of a loss of sensitivity due to increased electrical noise at higher temperatures, the increased energy gap of high-temperature superconductors would offer sensitive detection in a largely inaccessible frequency range, and the simplified refrigeration allows increased ease of use. Other microwave applications include high-Q waveguides, phase shifters, and antenna arrays.

Analog Signal Processors

High-speed analog signal processors performing such functions as filtering, convolution, correlation, Fourier transformation, and analog-to-digital (A-to-D) conversion are important for many applications. Various high-speed A-to-D converters have been tested successfully at 4.2 K. If high-quality Josephson junctions can be fabricated from the new superconductors, these devices should perform comparably at 77 K. At this temperature, integration of the superconducting devices with some semiconducting devices (for example, complementary metal-oxide semiconductors) becomes feasible, and new hybrid systems may well result in the fastest A-to-D converters available.

Magnetic Shielding

Both superconducting wires and superconducting sheets have been used for many years to create regions free from all magnetic fields or to shape magnetic fields. The advent of high-temperature superconductors may extend the range of this application. Like niobium-tin, high-temperature superconductors may be plasma-sprayed, permitting their use on surfaces of complex shape.

Voltage Standard

Many countries now maintain a voltage standard in terms of the voltage generated across a low-temperature superconducting Josephson junction irradiated by microwaves at a precise frequency. This standard could be more cheaply maintained and more widely available with no significant loss of accuracy by operating at 77 K with the new materials.

THE PRESENT MARKET FOR SUPERCONDUCTORS AND LIKELY CHANGES ASSOCIATED WITH THE NEW MATERIALS

The world superconductor industry is small, but superconducting devices are usually components of larger systems whose gross annual sales volume is many times the value of the devices themselves. Annual device sales total about $400 million, of which medical imaging machines and electronics instruments each account for approximately $150 million. Magnet coils represent 10 to 20 percent of device costs in MRI systems, and annual sales of basic materials such as alloy rod and sheet are on the order of $10–$20 million.

It is difficult to estimate the potential economic impact of today's high-temperature superconductors because so little is known about them and much depends on improved understanding and technological development. Assuming that satisfactory conductors can be manufactured, there are considerable advantages to operation in liquid nitrogen. Refrigeration units are simpler and cost less to operate. Conductor stability generally improves as the temperature increases because of the higher heat capacity of materials; however, the protective effect of the shunting normal conductor is reduced slightly because of its increased resistivity. Structural materials are less brittle at higher temperatures; therefore, more conventional structures can be used. Cryogenic liquids and systems, however, will still be needed. In comparing superconductor technology with present room temperature devices, the need for cooling is a serious economic and technological disadvantage. There is a great difference between switching on a machine as needed and having to supply continuous refrigeration, or having to wait for refrigeration systems to reach operating temperatures.

Assuming that some utility and heavy

electric power applications can be competitively marketed using systems cooled by liquid nitrogen, the superconducting materials market may be substantially increased; the market for heavy electrical equipment, however, would be mainly a replacement one, because few new systems are being built.

For substantial business growth above that projected for low-temperature superconductors, new technology developments are needed. There is little doubt that the new materials offer technological advantages, for they promise high-magnetic-field devices and new types of electronic sensors and switches at lower refrigeration costs than before. The panel is unanimous in stating that advances are bound to result in new applications and new economic growth. If room temperature superconductors become available, we can confidently expect a truly revolutionary expansion of superconducting applications in electrotechnology.

THE GLOBAL PICTURE: SUPERCONDUCTIVITY CAPABILITIES IN OTHER COUNTRIES

On a global scale, today's world superconductor industry is small but mature and principally confined to the developed countries. Basic research capabilities are more widespread.

Although much of the early impetus for research and development came from the United States, technology transfer has not been unidirectional. National and international conferences on all aspects of low-temperature physics have become routine.

Over the past 25 years, in several countries a wide variety of applications of superconducting electrotechnology have been examined in prototype development programs. No replacements for conventional applications have reached the market, however. As a result the demand for superconducting materials has been relatively small and has lacked continuity, being largely oriented toward development. Nevertheless, in most countries, government programs have supported a fledgling industry.

In the United States, magnet development for high-energy physics machines has been carried out in the national laboratories. Fusion and MHD magnets have been built both in the national laboratories and in private industry. There is also a rapidly growing commercial market based mainly on new medical imaging systems. A small materials and wire industry serves magnet development efforts. Many U.S. firms have supported their own research and development efforts in superconductor technology, both for power and electronic applications. A few small, continuing ventures have succeeded in superconducting electronics; a large market for superconducting electronic devices or systems has not yet developed.

Corporations in Europe and Japan have also fostered and maintained an expertise in superconductivity. In those nations, foreign governments have to some degree protected their superconductor industries by ensuring that equipment for government laboratories is built by domestic private industry; foreign bids are not accepted, a policy that ensures national industrial expertise. By comparison, much of this work in the United States is carried out in the federal laboratories from which there is little transfer to industry. In addition, foreign superconductor firms are allowed to bid on equipment needed by the United States government.

The USSR also has aggressive, long-term programs in energy conservation (including superconducting power transmission and storage), fabrication of superconducting wires and tapes, electronics, collider construction, magnetic fusion, magnetohydrodynamics, and superconducting generators.

Over the years, the United States has provided world leadership in superconducting science and technology, and has generously shared its own technology with other nations. Current collaborative efforts include the International Large Coil Fusion Project at Oak Ridge National Laboratory and Japanese development of a very large detector magnet for the Fermilab collider interaction area. In the evaluation of conductors for the physics collider magnets (the Superconducting Super Collider and the heavy-ion collider), material has been purchased from Japanese and European firms. The United States, through Brookhaven National Laboratory, also provides test evaluations of cables and conductors for the Hadron Electron Ring Accelerator (HERA) collider under construction in Hamburg, West Germany. Two prototype magnets for the Relativistic Heavy-Ion Collider (RHIC) have been purchased from the Brown Boveri Corporation (West Germany) because this was the cheapest and quickest way to obtain them (Brown Boveri had the necessary tooling because of their work for HERA).

BASIC HIGH-TEMPERATURE SUPERCONDUCTING RESEARCH

Basic research in high-temperature superconductivity is being actively pursued in all of the developed nations mentioned above and in several developing nations. In most cases scientists have switched spontaneously from other scientific activities into high-temperature superconductivity research. To this point, however, little new money has gone into basic research efforts. Plans are being prepared for 1988, but at present no major new government resources have been committed. The prevailing attitude appears to be that of waiting to see how the science progresses.

In *Japan* the scientific and technical community has responded vigorously, but aside from reprogramming there has been modest immediate additional action by government agencies. The latter have, however, been quite active in formulating plans for the next fiscal year (which begins in April 1988). Private industrial corporations are said to be investing their own funds heavily in research

on high-temperature superconductors, with the government intervening to establish industry consortia to pursue prototyping and other early development activities. Japan offers perhaps the strongest long-range competitive threat to the U.S. position.

In *Europe*, historical strengths in basic research and industrial development are being applied to the new superconductors. National and cross-national efforts are in the early organizational stages at best (again, with the exception of the reprogramming of research funds), and major project goals to drive technical problem solving are not yet in place. On the other hand, a variety of industrial corporations are involved in research, and precompetitive collaborations appear to be at advanced planning stages.

In the *USSR*, traditional scientific strengths in superconductivity theory and basic experimental approaches are being applied to the new materials. In addition, work is being carried out on the susceptibility of high-temperature superconducting materials to radiation damage.

SUMMARY OF PANEL VIEWS AND RECOMMENDATIONS

STATUS OF SCIENCE AND TECHNOLOGY

• The discovery of materials that exhibit superconductivity at temperatures up to 95 K is a major scientific event, certainly one of the more important of the last decade. Meeting the complex challenge of understanding the phenomenon will improve fundamental knowledge of the electronic properties of solids.

• Although a large number of promising theories are being explored, there is as yet no generally accepted theoretical explanation of the high critical temperature behavior. Current theoretical understanding does not preclude T_cs above 95 K.

• The base of experimental knowledge on the new superconductors is growing rapidly. The intrinsic properties that can guide theory are still being determined. A number of investigators have reported superconducting-like transitions at temperatures above 95 K, in some cases even above room temperature; at present those effects have not been firmly established.

• The prospect exists for applying the new superconductors to both electrical and electronic technology. The nature of the new materials (quaternary ceramic oxides) suggests that a substantial materials engineering effort will be required to develop bulk conductors for power applications or thin films for electronic applications.

• The applications currently being considered are largely extrapolations of technology already under investigation for lower temperature superconductors. To create a larger scope of applications, inventions that use the new materials will be required. Given the materials engineering problems already mentioned, the period of precommercial exploration of the new superconductors for other applications will probably last for a decade or more. Although it is too early to make a sound engineering judgment about most of the possible high-temperature superconductivity applications, the potential impact could be enormous, especially if operation at room temperature can be achieved.

• Near-term prospects for high-temperature-superconductivity applications include magnetic shielding, the voltage standard, SQUIDs, infrared sensors, microwave devices, and analog signal processing. Longer-term prospects include large-scale applications such as microwave cavities; power transmission lines; and superconducting magnets in generators, energy storage devices, particle accelerators, rotating machinery, medical imaging systems, levitated vehicles, and magnetic separators. In electronics, long-term prospects include computer applications with semiconducting-superconducting hybrids, Josephson devices, or novel transistor-like superconducting devices. Several of these technologies will have military applications.

• The complexity of the materials technology and of many of these applications makes a long-term view of research and development essential for success in commercialization. The infectious enthusiasm in the press and elsewhere may have contributed to premature public expectations of revolutionary technology on a very short time scale. Overreaction in either direction could be detrimental to achieving the true long-term potential of high-temperature superconductivity.

The United States and the World Situation

• Although the initial high-temperature superconductivity discovery was made in the Swiss research laboratory of IBM, the next advances occurred very soon afterward in the United States. These advances were the synthesis of 1-2-3 compounds with T_cs of up to 95 K. Before the constituents of the material were known, independent discoveries of the superconducting behavior of these compounds were also made in China and Japan a few days later.

• The United States has a good competitive position in the science of this field. It has also shown flexibility; scientists in universities and industrial and government laboratories have spontaneously switched into this field from their previous endeavors and have contributed significantly to the worldwide expansion of scientific knowledge on the new superconductors. Nevertheless, there is concern about the effectiveness of the nation's capabilities for translating this research strength into commercial products.

• The U.S. government has already reprogrammed close to $30 million of research funds for high-temperature superconductivity work in universities and industrial laboratories for fiscal year 1987. We estimate that at least an equivalent amount of private funds are being expended by U.S. corporations. Total annual funding levels will probably be in the range of $100–$200 million by 1988, although firm figures for industry are not available.

• These expenditures will expand the U.S. graduate and postgraduate population working in areas relevant to high-temperature superconductivity and will create pressures on the nation's scientific manpower pool.

• The rapid dissemination of scientific results has occurred mainly through word of mouth, preprints, and press releases, reflecting the close-knit global community of scientific endeavor. At present there are hardly any restrictions on the flow of information throughout the world.

• International competition in high-temperature superconductivity is intense. The leading industrialized countries, especially the United States, Japan, several Western European countries, and the USSR have mounted substantial scientific and technological efforts.

• Should successful technologies emerge from the discoveries in high-temperature superconductivity, the United States has many of the ingredients needed to develop and commercialize those technologies. Whether this will result in business success for U.S. corporations in the global market will depend not only on technological factors but also on company business strategies and a range of government policies. The panel is not qualified to address these latter issues comprehensively but has made some recommendations, listed below, that should assist commercialization.

FURTHER PROGRESS: THE NEXT STEPS

The short-term problems and long-term potential of high-temperature superconductivity may both be easily underestimated. Given this potential and today's limited understanding of the new superconducting materials and their properties, it is essential that government, academic institutions, and industry take a long-term, multidisciplinary view. Because science and technology in this field are strongly intertwined, progress must occur simultaneously in basic science, manufacturing processing science, and engineering applications. It is also important to maintain an open and cooperative international posture.

Scientific and Technological Objectives

The panel has identified eight major scientific and technological objectives for a national program to exploit high-temperature superconductivity. They are:

1. to improve understanding of the essential properties of current high-temperature superconducting materials (especially T_c, H_{c2}, J_c, and alternating current losses) through the acquisition of additional experimental data;

2. to develop an understanding of the basic mechanisms responsible for superconductivity in the new materials;

3. to search for additional materials exhibiting superconductivity at higher temperatures by the synthesis of new compositions, structures, and phases;

4. to prepare thin films of controllable and reproducible quality from present high-temperature superconducting materials, and establish preferred techniques for growing films suitable for electronic device fabrication;

5. to develop bulk conductors from current high-temperature superconducting materials, with special emphasis on enhanced electric current-carrying capacity;

6. to advance the understanding of the chemistry, chemical engineering, and ceramic properties of the new materials, focusing on synthesis, processing, stability, and methods for large-scale production;

7. to fabricate a range of prototype circuits and electronic devices based on superconducting microcircuits or hybrid supercon-

ductor/semiconductor circuits, as suitable thin film technologies become available; and

8. to fabricate a range of prototype high-field magnets, alternating- and direct-current power devices, rotating machines, transmission circuits, and energy storage devices, as suitable bulk conductors are developed.

PANEL RECOMMENDATIONS

The panel recommends that the following actions be taken to carry out the objectives listed above:

• The U.S. government should proceed with its plans to provide funding for high-temperature superconductivity research and development on the order of $100 million for fiscal year 1988. This funding level represents a good beginning in addressing the challenges and opportunities offered by the new materials.

• Sufficient new money must be provided to both the science and the technology of high-temperature superconductivity so that other important and promising areas of research and development are not held back.

• A mechanism should be established to monitor the potential demand for increased scientific and technical manpower in the event that the promise of high-temperature superconductivity is fully realized, and to formulate appropriate recommendations on the funding of U.S. graduate and postgraduate research programs.

• An interagency mechanism should be established to help coordinate planning for superconductivity programs among the various federal agencies.

• Given the anticipated rate of advance in high-temperature superconducting science and technology, the federal government should review progress in the field after 12 months as a guide to future resource allocation.

• Through its agencies the U.S. government must enhance the probability that U.S. industry gains a competitive advantage in this new field. This could be accomplished by the close association of industry with the Engineering Research or Science and Technology Center programs of the National Science Foundation, by cost-sharing between government and industry on proof-of-concept projects, and by other joint efforts.

• An important mechanism for enhancing U.S. industry's position is improved technology transfer from the national laboratories to the private sector. Although a variety of means are already in place to encourage such transfers, the panel is concerned about the effectiveness of past efforts and urges both government and industry to pursue linkages more aggressively.

Report of the
Research Briefing Panel on
Chemical Processing of Materials and
Devices for Information Storage
and Handling

Research Briefing Panel on Chemical Processing of Materials and Devices for Information Storage and Handling

Larry F. Thompson (*Chairman*), Head,
Organic Materials and Chemical
Engineering, AT&T Bell Laboratories

Lee L. Blyler, Supervisor, Plastics Applied
Research, Properties, and Processing,
AT&T Bell Laboratories

James Economy, Manager, Polymer Science
and Technology, IBM Almaden Research
Center

Dennis W. Hess, Professor of Chemical
Engineering, University of California,
Berkeley

Richard Pollard, Professor of Chemical
Engineering, University of Houston

T. W. Fraser Russell, Professor of Chemical
Engineering, University of Delaware

Michael Sheptak, Senior Staff Engineer,
Magnetic Tape Division, Ampex
Corporation

Staff

Robert M. Simon, *Project Director*, Board on
Chemical Sciences and Technology

Allan R. Hoffman, *Executive Director*,
Committee on Science, Engineering, and
Public Policy

Report of the
Research Briefing Panel on
Chemical Processing of Materials and
Devices for Information Storage
and Handling

INTRODUCTION

Almost every aspect of our lives—at work, at home, and in recreation—has been affected by the information revolution. Today, information is collected, processed, displayed, stored, retrieved, and transmitted through the use of an array of powerful technologies that rely on electronic microcircuits, lightwave communication systems, magnetic and optical data storage and recording, and electrical interconnections. Materials and devices for these technologies are manufactured using sophisticated chemical processes. The United States is now engaged in a fierce international competition to achieve and maintain supremacy in the design and manufacture of materials and devices for information storage and processing. The economic stakes are large (see Table 1); national productivity and security interests dictate that we make the strongest possible efforts to stay ahead in processing science and technology for this area.

This briefing explores the chemical processing required in three of these key technologies: electronic microcircuits, lightwave communication systems, and magnetic recording media. This briefing also explores briefly some potential needs for advanced chemical processing that may be required to realize more fully the promise of superconducting metal oxides.

In high-technology manufacturing of components for information systems, there has been a long-term trend away from mechanical production and toward production using chemical processes. In several of these industries, chemists and chemical engineers have become increasingly involved in research and process development. Worldwide, though, many high-technology industries, such as the microelectronics industry, still have surprisingly little strength in chemical processing and engineering. The United States has a special advantage over its international competitors—its chemical engineering research community leads the world in size and sophistication. The United States is in a position to exploit its strong competence in chemical processing to (1) regain leadership in areas in which the initiative in manufacturing technology has passed to Japan, and (2) maintain or increase leadership in areas of U.S. technological strength.

To achieve their potential contribution fully, it is of paramount importance that chemical engineers strongly interact with

27

TABLE 1 Total Estimated Worldwide Market for Materials and Devices for Information Storage and Handling (billions of 1986 dollars)

Technology	Year		
	1985	1990	1995
Electronic semicon-ductors	25	60	160
Lightwaves	1	3	5.5
Recording materials	7	20	55
Interconnections	10	21	58
Photovoltaics	0.3	0.8	3
Total Electronics	397	550	(n.a)

Source: AT&T Bell Laboratories.
Compiled from various published sources.

other disciplines in high-technology industries and have the ability to communicate across disciplinary lines. The technologies discussed in this report cross over disciplines such as solid-state physics and chemistry, surface and interfacial science, electrical engineering, and materials science.

Materials and devices for information storage and handling are exceedingly diverse, yet they have many characteristics in common: the products are high in value; they require relatively small amounts of energy or materials to manufacture; they have short commercial life cycles; and their markets are fiercely competitive—consequently, these products experience rapid price erosion. The manufacturing methods used to produce integrated circuits, optical fiber, and recording media also have common characteristics. Each of these products is manufactured using a sequence of individual, complex steps, most of which entail the chemical modification or synthesis of materials. The individual processes are designed as discrete unit or batch operations and, to date, there has been little effort to integrate the overall manufacturing process. Because chemical reactions and processes are used in the manufacture of this broad array of materials and devices,

chemical engineers could play a significant role in improving manufacturing processes and techniques, and investments in chemical processing science and engineering research represent a potentially high-leverage approach to improving our competitive position.

CURRENT CHEMICAL MANUFACTURING PROCESSES

MICROCIRCUITS

The use of chemical reactions and processes in the manufacture of microcircuits begins with the basic material for integrated circuits, high-purity (less than 150 parts per trillion of impurities) polycrystalline silicon. This ultrapure silicon is produced from metallurgical grade (98 percent pure) silicon, by (1) reaction at high temperature with hydrogen chloride to form a complex mixture containing trichlorosilane; (2) separation and purification of trichlorosilane by absorption and distillation; and (3) reduction of ultrapure trichlorosilane to polycrystalline silicon by reaction with hydrogen at 1100–1200°C. To prepare single-crystal silicon ingots suitable for use as materials in semiconductors, polycrystalline silicon is melted in a crucible at 1400–1500°C under an argon atmosphere. Tiny quantities of dopants—compounds of phosphorus, arsenic, or boron—are then added to the melt to achieve the desired electrical properties of the finished single-crystal wafers. A tiny seed crystal of silicon with the proper crystalline orientation is inserted into the melt and slowly rotated and withdrawn at a precisely controlled rate, forming a large (15 cm × 1.8 m) cylindrical single crystal with the desired crystalline orientation and composition. Crystal growth kinetics, heat and mass transfer relationships, and chemical reactions all play important roles in this process of controlled growth. The resulting single-crystal ingots are sawed into wafers that are polished to a flatness in the range of from 1 to 10 μm.

The next steps in device fabrication are the sequential deposition and patterning of thin dielectric and conducting films. The polished silicon wafer is first oxidized in a furnace at 1000–1200°C. The resultant silicon dioxide film is a few hundred nanometers thick and extremely uniform. The wafer is then coated with an organic photosensitive material, termed a resist, and is exposed to light through the appropriate photomask. The purpose of the photolithographic process is to transfer the mask pattern to the thin film on the wafer surface. The exposed organic film is developed with a solvent that removes unwanted portions, and the resulting pattern serves as a mask for chemically etching the pattern into the silicon dioxide film. The resist is then removed with an oxidizing agent such as a sulfuric acid-hydrogen peroxide mixture, then the wafer is chemically cleaned and is ready for other steps in the fabrication process.

The patterned wafer might next be placed in a diffusion furnace, where a first doping step is performed to deposit phosphorus or boron into the holes in the oxide. A new oxide film can then be grown and the photoresist process repeated. As many as 12 layers of conductor, semiconductor, and dielectric materials are deposited, etched, and/or doped to build the three-dimensional structure of the microcircuit. Thus a semiconductor device is a series of electrically interconnected films, the successful growth and manipulation of which depends heavily on proper reactor design, the choice of chemical reagents, separation and purification steps, and the design and operation of sophisticated control systems.

LIGHTWAVE MEDIA AND DEVICES

Optical fibers are also made by chemical processes. The critical feature of an optical fiber that allows it to propagate light down its length is a core of high refractive index surrounded by a cladding of lower index. The higher index core is produced by doping silica with oxides of phosphorus, germanium, and/or aluminum. The cladding is either pure silica or silica doped with fluorides or boron oxide.

Four processes are principally used to manufacture the glass body that is drawn into today's optical fiber. "Outside" processes, such as outside vapor-phase oxidation and vertical axial deposition, produce layered deposits of doped silica by varying the concentration of $SiCl_4$ and dopants passing through a torch. The resulting "soot" of doped silica is deposited and partially sintered to form a porous silica boule. In a second step, the boule is sintered to a pore-free glass rod of exquisite purity and transparency. "Inside" processes, such as modified chemical vapor deposition (MCVD) and plasma chemical vapor deposition (PCVD), deposit doped silica on the interior surface of a fused silica tube. In MCVD, the oxidation of the halide reactants is initiated by a flame that heats the outside of the tube. In PCVD, the reaction is initiated by a microwave plasma. Over a hundred different layers with different refractive indexes (a function of glass composition) may be deposited by either process before the tube is collapsed to form a glass rod.

In current manufacturing plants for glass fiber, the glass rods formed by all of the abovementioned processes are then carried to another facility where they are drawn into a thin fiber and immediately coated with a polymer. The polymer coating is important; it protects the fiber surface from microscopic scratches, which can seriously degrade the glass fiber's strength.

Current manufacturing technologies for optical fiber are relatively expensive, compared to the low cost of commodity glass. U.S. economic competitiveness in optical technologies would be greatly enhanced if low-cost means were found for producing waveguide-quality silica glass. The manufacture of glass lends itself to a fully integrated and automated process (i.e., a continuous process). One can envision a fiber manufacturing plant that starts with the purification of chemical reagents, which is then followed by a series of chemical reactions, glass-forming operations, and finally fiber-drawing steps. In such a plant, intermediate products would never be removed from the "production line." Sol–gel and related processes are attractive candidates for such a manufacturing process, which would start with inexpensive ingredients and proceed from a sol to a gel, to a porous silica body, to a dried and sintered glass rod, and finally to drawn and coated fibers. Such a process could reduce the cost of glass fiber by as much as a factor of 10, a step that would greatly increase the scope, availability, and competitiveness of lightwave technologies.

At present the chemical steps involved in sol–gel processes are poorly understood. Methods are being sought to manipulate these processes to produce precisely layered structures in a reliable and reproducible way.

RECORDING MEDIA

Recording media come in a variety of formats (e.g., magnetic tape, magnetic disks, or optical disks) and are made using a variety of materials and processes (e.g., evaporated thin films or deposited magnetic particles in polymer matrixes). To illustrate the chemical reactions and processes in the manufacture of recording media, this section focuses on magnetic particle technology, an economically important part of the market for which the processing challenges are easy to discuss. Chemical reactions and processes are equally relevant to emerging technologies and materials in recording.

The manufacture of magnetic recording media depends heavily on chemical processing. The density at which information can be recorded is determined by the chemical and physical properties of the magnetic particles or thin films coated on a disk or tape. Paramount among these properties are the shape, size, and size distribution of the magnetic particles. An extremely narrow range in the size of magnetic particles—themselves only a few tenths of a micron in size—must be achieved in a reliable and economic manner. These particles must be deposited in a highly oriented fashion, so that high recording densities can be achieved by having the magnetic particles lie as closely together as possible. Accomplishing this requires the solution of a variety of challenging problems in the chemistry and chemical engineering of barium ferrite and the oxides of chromium, cobalt, and iron (e.g., the synthesis and processing of micron-sized materials with specific geometric shapes).

The manufacture of magnetic tape illustrates an interesting sequence of chemical processing challenges. A carefully prepared dispersion of needle-like magnetic particles is coated onto a fast-moving (150–300 m/min) polyester film base that is 0.0066- to 0.08-mm thick. The ability to coat thin, smooth layers of uniform thickness is crucial. The coated particles are oriented in a desired direction either magnetically or mechanically during the coating process. After drying, the tape is calendared—squeezed between microsmooth steel and polymer rolls that rotate at different rates, providing a "microslip" action that polishes the tape surface. These manufacturing steps (i.e., materials synthesis, preparation and handling of uniform dispersions, coating, drying, and calendaring) are chemical processes and/or unit operations that are familiar territory to chemical engineering analysis and design.

INTERNATIONAL COMPETITIVE ASSESSMENT

INTRODUCTION

In each of the technologies described in the preceding section, U.S. leadership in both fundamental research and manufacturing is severely challenged, and in some cases the United States has been judged to lag behind foreign competitors such as Japan.

MICROCIRCUITS

A recent report of the National Research Council* has assessed the comparative position of the United States and Japan in advanced processing of electronic materials. The report, which focuses heavily on evaluating Japanese research on specific process steps in the manufacture of electronic materials, provides significant background for the following observations.

• The U.S. electronics industry appears to be ahead of, or on a par with, Japanese industry in most areas of current techniques for the deposition and processing of thin films—chemical vapor deposition (CVD), metalorganic chemical vapor deposition (MOCVD), and molecular beam epitaxy (MBE). There are differences in some areas, though, that may be crucial to future technologies. For example, the Japanese effort in low-pressure microwave plasma research is impressive and surpasses the U.S. effort in some respects. The Japanese are ahead of their U.S. counterparts in the design and manufacture of deposition equipment, as well.

• Japanese industry has a very substantial commitment to advancing high-resolution lithography at the fastest possible pace. Two Japanese companies, Nikon and Canon, have made significant inroads at the cutting edge of optical lithography equipment. In the fields of x-ray and electron-beam lithography, it appears that U.S. equipment manufacturers have lost the initiative to Japan for the development of commercial equipment.

• Japanese researchers are ahead of their U.S. counterparts in the application of laser and electron beams and solid-phase epitaxy for the fabrication of silicon-on-insulator structures.

• The United States leads in basic research related to implantation processes and in the development of equipment for conventional applications of ion implantation. Japan appears to have the initiative in the development of equipment for ion microbeam technologies.

Neither the United States nor Japan has satisfactorily solved the problems of process integration in microcircuit manufacture. As the previous comparisons indicate, much effort is being expended on equipment design for specific processing steps, but a parallel effort to integrate the processing of these materials across the many individual steps has received less attention in both countries. Yet the latter effort might have significant payoffs in improved process reliability and efficiency—that is, in "manufacturability." The United States has the capability to take a significant lead in this area.

LIGHTWAVE TECHNOLOGY

The Japanese are our prime competitors in the development of lightwave technology. They are not dominant in the manufacture of optical fiber thanks in part to a strong overlay of patents on basic manufacturing processes by U.S. companies. In fact, a major Japanese company manufactures optical fiber in North Carolina for shipment to Japan. This is the only example to date of Japan importing a high-technology product from a U.S. subsidiary. Nonetheless, the Japanese are making strong efforts to surpass the United States, and are reaching a par with the United States in many areas.

The United States still significantly leads Japan in producing special purpose and high-strength fibers, in preparing cables from groups of fibers, and in research on hermetic coatings for fibers.

RECORDING MEDIA

Japan is the United States' principal technological competitor in the manufacture of

---

* Panel on Materials Science, National Materials Advisory Board. *Advanced Processing of Electronic Materials in the United States and Japan.* Washington, D.C.: National Academy Press, 1986.

magnetic media, and Korean firms are beginning to make significant inroads at the low end of the market for magnetic tape. U.S. companies producing magnetic tape use manufacturing processes that achieve higher integration through combined unit operations, but Japanese companies have a higher degree of automation in these separate operations. U.S. companies are ahead of the Japanese in the use of newer thermoplastics in calendar-compliant roll materials. Japan used to surpass the United States in the product uniformity of magnetic tape for professional applications; U.S. firms have closed this gap in recent years, and are now capturing worldwide market share from the Japanese, even in Japan.

The most significant development in Japan is the entry of photographic film companies (i.e., Fuji and Konishuroku) into the manufacture of magnetic media. They are having a large impact because the heart of the manufacturing process is the deposition of thin layers, and chemical processing technology from the photographic film business can be used to improve the quality and yield of magnetic tape.

The United States still lags behind Japan in the treatment and manufacture of magnetic particles (except possibly for 3M, which manufactures its particles internally). There are disturbing signs that the Japanese may be ahead of the United States in the next generation of film base, especially the film base for vapor-deposition magnetic media. The situation is not entirely clear, because 3M and Kodak make their own proprietary film. Other U.S. magnetic media companies, though, may be buying their film technology from Japan in the future.

General Observations

As noted previously, the industries that manufacture high-technology materials and components for information processing and storage are characterized by short product life cycles, enormous competition, and rapid erosion of product value. These industries also need rapid technology transfer from the research laboratory onto the production line. Many of their *products* cannot be protected by patents, except for minor features. The key to their competitive success is thoroughly characterized and integrated manufacturing *processes*, supported by process innovations. In the past, much of the process technology on which these industries depend has been developed empirically. If the United States is to maintain a competitive position in these industries, it is essential that we develop the fundamental knowledge necessary to stimulate further improvement of, and innovation in, processes involving chemical reactions that must be precisely controlled in a manufacturing environment. In the next section the principal technical challenges are set forth.

GENERIC RESEARCH ISSUES

Introduction

A variety of important research issues are ripe for a substantially increased effort to enable U.S. companies to establish and maintain dominance in information storage and handling technologies. These research issues are quite broad and cut across the spectrum of materials and devices.

Process Integration

Process integration is the key challenge in the design of efficient and cost-effective manufacturing processes for electronic, photonic, and recording materials and devices. Currently, these products are manufactured by a series of individual, isolated steps. If the United States is to retain a position of leadership, it is crucial that the overall manufacturing methodology be examined and integrated manufacturing approaches be implemented. Historically, all industries have benefited both economically and in the quality and yield of products by the use of integrated manufacturing methods. As individual process steps become more complex and precise, the final results of manufacturing (e.g., yield, throughput, and reliability) often depend critically on the interactions among the various steps. Thus, it becomes increasingly important to automate and integrate individual process steps into an overall manufacturing process.

The concepts of chemical engineering are easily applied in meeting the challenge of process integration, particularly because many of the key process steps involve chemical reactions. For example, in the manufacture of microcircuits, chemical engineers can provide mathematical models and control algorithms for the transient and steady-state operation of individual chemical process steps (e.g., lithography, etching, film deposition, diffusion, and oxidation), as well as models and associated control algorithms for the interactions between one process step and another, and ultimately between processing and the characteristics of the final device. As another example, in microcircuit manufacture, chemical engineers can provide needed simulations of the dynamics of material movement through the plant, and thus optimize the flow of devices (or wafers) through a fabrication line.

REACTOR ENGINEERING AND DESIGN

Closely related to challenges in process integration are research challenges in reactor engineering and design. Research in this area is important if we are to automate manufacturing processes for higher yields and improved product quality. Contributions from chemical engineers are needed to meet this challenge—processes such as CVD, epitaxy, plasma-enhanced CVD, plasma-enhanced etching, reactive sputtering, and oxidation all take place in chemical reactors. At present, these processes and reactors are generally developed and optimized by trial and error. A basic understanding of fundamental phenomena and reactor design in

these areas would facilitate process design, control, and reliability. Because each of these processes involves reaction kinetics, mass transfer, and fluid flow, chemical engineers can bring a rich background to the study and improvement of these processes.

An important consideration in reactor design and engineering is the ultraclean storage and transfer of chemicals. This is not a trivial problem; generally, the containers and transfer media are the primary sources of contamination in manufacturing. Methods are needed for storing gases and liquids, for purifying them (see the next section), and for delivering them to the equipment where they will be used—all the while maintaining impurity levels below 1 part per billion. This purity requirement puts severe constraints on the types of materials that can be used in handling chemicals. For example, materials in reactor construction that might be chosen primarily on the basis of safety often cannot be used. Designs are needed that will meet the multiple objectives of high purity, safety, and low cost.

The ultimate limit to the size of microelectronic devices is that of molecular dimensions. The ability to "tailor" films at the molecular level—to deposit a film and control its properties by altering or forming the structure, atomic layer by atomic layer—opens exciting possibilities for new types of devices and structures. The fabrication of these multilayer, multimaterial structures will require more sophisticated deposition methods, such as MBE and MOCVD. Depositing uniform films by these methods over large dimensions will require reactors with a different design than those currently used, especially for epitaxial growth processes. The challenge is to be able to control the flow of reactants to build layered structures tens of atoms thick (e.g., superlattices). To achieve economic automated processes, the reactor design has to allow for the acquisition of detailed real-time information on the surface processes taking place, fed back into an exquisite control system and reagent delivery system. This problem gives rise to an exciting series of basic research topics.

ULTRAPURIFICATION

A third research challenge that is generic to electronic, photonic, and recording materials and devices stems from the need for starting materials that meet purity levels once thought to be unattainable.

This need is particularly acute for semiconductor materials and optical fibers. For semiconductor materials, the challenge is to find new, lower cost routes to ultrapure silicon and gallium arsenide, and to purify other reagents used in the manufacturing process so that they do not introduce particulate contamination or other defects into the device being manufactured. For optical fibers, precursor materials of high purity are also needed. For example, the $SiCl_4$ currently used in optical fiber manufacture must have a total of less than 5 parts per million of hydrogen-containing compounds and less than 2 parts per billion of metal compounds. Either impurity will result in strong light absorption in the glass fiber. For magnetic media, the challenge is to separate and purify submicron-sized magnetic particles to very exacting size and shape tolerances.

A variety of separation research topics have a bearing on these needs. These include generating improved selectivity in separations by tailoring the chemical and steric interactions of separating agents, understanding and exploiting interfacial phenomena in separations, improving the rate and capacity of separations, and finding improved process configurations for separations. These are all research issues central to chemical engineering.

CHEMICAL SYNTHESIS AND PROCESSING OF CERAMIC MATERIALS

The traditional approach to creating and processing ceramics has been through the grinding, mixing, and sintering of powders.

Although still useful in some applications, this technology is being replaced by approaches that rely on chemical reactions to create a uniform microstructure. Among the typical examples of such an approach would be sol–gel and related processes. A tremendous opportunity exists for chemists and chemical engineers to apply their detailed knowledge of fundamental chemical processes in developing new chemical routes to high-performance ceramics for electronic and photonic applications.

Deeper involvement of chemical engineers in manufacturing processes for ceramics may be particularly important in the eventual commercialization of metal oxide superconductors. The current generation of such superconductors consist of structures that are formed during a conventional ceramic synthesis. It is by no means clear that the structures that may produce optimal performance in such superconducting ceramics (e.g., room-temperature superconductivity, capacity for high current density) are accessible by these techniques. Rational synthesis of structured ceramics by chemical processing may be crucial to further improvements in superconducting properties and in affording efficient large-scale production.

DEPOSITION OF THIN FILMS

Precise and reproducible deposition of thin films is another area of great importance in the chemical processing of materials and devices for the information age.

In microelectronic devices, there is a steady trend toward decreasing pattern sizes, and by the end of this decade the smallest pattern size on production circuits will be less than 1 μm. Although the lithographic tools to print such patterns exist, the exposure step is only one of a number of processes that must be performed sequentially in a mass production environment without creating defects. Precise and uniform deposition of materials as very thin films onto substrates 15 cm or more in diameter must be performed in a reactor, usually at reduced pressure. Particulate defects larger than 0.1 μm in these films must be virtually nonexistent. Low-temperature methods of film deposition will be needed so that defects are not generated in previous or neighboring films by unwanted diffusion of dopants.

For optical fibers, improved control over the structure of the thin films in the preform will lead to fibers with improved radial gradients of refractive index. A particular challenge might be to achieve this sort of control in preforms created using sol–gel or related processes.

Another challenge in depositing thin films on optical fibers occurs in the final coating step. Improved coating materials that can be cured very rapidly, for example, by ultraviolet radiation, are needed for high-speed (> 10 m/s) fiber-drawing processes. Both glassy and elastomeric polymers with low glass transition temperatures are needed for use over temperatures ranging from −60 to 85°C or higher. Hermetic coatings are required to avoid water-induced stress corrosion of silica glasses, which proceeds by slow crack growth. Materials under study include silicon carbide and titanium carbide applied by chemical vapor deposition, as well as metals such as aluminum. A 10-fold increase in the rate at which such coatings can be applied to silica fiber during drawing is needed for commercial success. These coatings must be pinhole-free, have low residual stress, and adhere well. Hermetic coatings will also be needed to protect the moisture-sensitive halide and chalcogenide glasses that may find use in optical fibers of the future because of their compatibility with transmission at longer wavelengths.

Considerable progress in the science and technology of depositing thin films is needed if the U.S. recording media industry is to remain competitive with foreign manufacturers. New, fully automated coating processes that will generate high-quality, low-defect media are needed. Not only must con-

siderable effort be mounted in designing hardware and production equipment, but it is also necessary to develop complex mathematical models to gain an understanding of the kinetic and thermodynamic properties of film coating, as well as the effect of non-Newtonian flow and polymer and fluid rheology. A better understanding of dispersion stability during drying, as well as of diffusion mechanisms that result in intermixing of sequential layers of macromolecules, is important.

MODELING AND THE STUDY OF CHEMICAL DYNAMICS

A challenge related to the problems of reactor design and engineering is the modeling and study of the fundamental chemistry occurring in manufacturing processes for semiconductors, optical fibers, and magnetic media. For example, mathematical models originally developed for continuously stirred tank reactors and plug-flow reactors are applicable to the reactors used for thin-film processing, and can be modified to elucidate ways in which thin-film reactors can be improved. Enabling these models to reach their full descriptive potential will require detailed studies of the fundamental chemical reactions occurring on surfaces and in the gas phase. For example, etching rates, etching selectivity, line profiles, deposited film structure, film bonding, and film properties are determined by a host of variables, including the promotion of surface reactions by ion, electron, or photon bombardment. The fundamental chemistry of these surface reactions is poorly understood, and accurate rate expressions are particularly needed for electron-impact reactions (i.e., dissociation, ionization, or excitation), ion–ion reactions, neutral–neutral reactions, and ion–neutral reactions. The scale and scope of the effort devoted in recent years to understanding catalytic processes needs to be given to research related to film deposition and plasma etching. Until a basic understanding is achieved of chemical reactions occurring at the surface and in the gas phase, it will be difficult to develop new etching systems.

Research related to this area has had a demonstrable impact on recent innovations in plasma processing. Five years ago, it was well known that a fluorine-containing plasma etches silicon at a rate significantly greater than the rate for SiO_2, thus offering significant advantages for fabricating integrated circuits. However, well-controlled processes could not be developed that would perform in a production environment. The work of chemical engineers in elucidating the relevant chemical reactions and their kinetics was crucial to the identification of the important chemical species in the etching process, their reaction pathways, and, in addition, to the discovery that the organic polymer photoresist contributed to plasma chemistry and selectivity in important ways. These studies led to new, improved plasma processes that are currently being used in production.

For magnetic media, mathematical models could enhance our fundamental understanding of the manufacturing processes used to make uniform high-purity magnetic particles. Models for the kinetics and mechanisms of reactions and an improved understanding of the thermodynamics of producing inorganic salts are required.

ENVIRONMENT AND SAFETY

Safety and environmental protection are extremely important concerns in all of the high-technology areas already discussed. They present demanding intellectual challenges. The manufacture of materials and devices for information handling and storage involves substantial quantities of toxic, corrosive, or pyrophoric chemicals (e.g., hydrides and halides of arsenic, boron, phosphorus, and silicon; hydrocarbons and organic chlorides, some of which are cancer suspect agents; and inorganic acids). Unfortunately, the industries involved in manu-

facturing these materials and devices have only recently begun to employ significant numbers of chemical professionals, and have suffered from a lack of expertise in the safe handling and disposal of dangerous chemicals. Recent studies in California indicate that the semiconductor industry has an occupational illness rate 3 times that of general manufacturing industries. Nearly half of these illnesses involve systemic poisoning from exposure to toxic materials. Problems with groundwater contamination in Santa Clara County, California, have also raised concerns about how well the semiconductor industry is equipped to handle waste management and disposal. If the semiconductor and other advanced material industries are to continue to prosper in the United States, it is important that the expertise of chemical engineers be applied to every aspect of chemical handling in manufacturing, from procurement through use to disposal.

RECOMMENDATIONS

Pursuing the research frontiers discussed in the preceding section will significantly benefit our national standard of living, defense, education, and trade balance. How can we best use resources to foster work in these areas, and to foster communication and collaboration among researchers in industrial, academic, and federal laboratories?

The following goals should be set for improving national research capabilities that will result in improved manufacturing processes for electronic, photonic, and recording materials and devices.

• Federal agencies involved in the support of basic materials research (for example, the National Science Foundation [NSF], the U.S. Department of Energy, and the U.S. Department of Defense) should consider undertaking new initiatives in the support of fundamental research addressing the generic intellectual issues in the chemical processing of electronic, photonic, and recording materials and devices (see the preceding section).

• It is particularly important to involve chemists and chemical engineers in research related to ceramic synthesis and processing. Researchers trained in traditional approaches to ceramic materials may not have the optimal background to pursue the new challenges in the molecular design, synthesis, and engineering of ceramics.

• Fundamental research and training to meet the needs of industry for chemical process engineers and scientists should be broadly based in many academic institutions, for two reasons. First, many of the research areas mentioned in the preceding section lend themselves to research groups led by single principal investigators or by small teams of two or three coprincipal investigators. The magnitude of support given to such research groups should be enhanced to provide access to the sophisticated instrumentation needed to pursue effective research on fundamental phenomena important to research areas such as separations, processing, and reactor design. Second, the demand from the electronics industry alone for personnel with chemical backgrounds is sufficiently large that the founding of a few large centers is not likely to meet the need. Some chemical engineering departments, for example, are reporting that up to a quarter of their baccalaureate graduates are being hired by electronics firms.

• University research, particularly in engineering, should be effectively coupled to industry through collaborative mechanisms. Industry has been the prime mover in advancing technology in materials and components for information storage and handling, and will remain so for the foreseeable future. It is important, then, for university research groups to develop and maintain good communication with counterpart research groups in industry. The NSF Engineering Research Centers program and Industry–University Cooperative Research program are two effec-

tive means to stimulate such communication and collaboration.

• A few of the existing NSF Engineering Research Centers are addressing research issues that touch on the topics covered in this briefing. Where appropriate, these centers should be encouraged to seek broader participation in their programs from chemical scientists and engineers.

• The current undergraduate curriculum in chemical engineering, although it provides an excellent conceptual base for graduates who move into the electronics industries, could be improved by the introduction of instructional material and example problems relevant to the challenges outlined in this briefing. This would not require the creation of new courses, but the provision of material to enrich existing ones. Seminal texts often serve to redefine the boundaries of a discipline and to direct teaching and research toward new frontiers. The NSF should create incentives for select researchers at the cutting edge of chemical engineering to write the next generation of textbooks for their field.

The existing network of programs in funding agencies do not address some important problems in the generation and transfer of expertise and ideas from the research laboratory to the production line. For the technologies discussed in this report, a key role in generating new process concepts and equipment is played by a large number of relatively small firms. These firms are generally not in a position to make financial contributions to Engineering Research Centers or to retain academic consultants, yet face important research problems in fundamental science and engineering that would benefit markedly from the insights of academic researchers. The United States could significantly boost its competitive position in the technologies discussed in this report by facilitating information transfer between academia and this segment of industry. The problem for funding agencies with an interest in promoting U.S. capabilities in this area is how to create incentives for academic researchers to seek out and forge links to the small firms that stand at the crucial step between laboratory research and production processes. Examples of two possible mechanisms that provide these incentives follow.

• Agencies such as the NSF could create a new sabbatical award for academic researchers to spend up to a year in the laboratory of a small process technology firm. The rationale for such a program would be both to provide a critical sector of U.S. advanced process technology firms with the latest insights from university research, and to provide university researchers with insights into the ways in which fundamental science and engineering can contribute to the practical problems of high-technology processing of materials and devices.

• A limited number of "incubator research programs," providing state-of-the-art facilities cohabited by researchers from advanced process technology firms and researchers in process engineering associated with universities, could be set up in close proximity to academic research campuses. Key to these programs would be the contribution by industry of high-quality research personnel, in lieu of providing financial support for academic research conducted under these programs. The government might provide a significant portion of the facility costs to those university applicants that could assemble a critical mass of researchers from their own departments and from high-technology firms. The concept of "incubators" is not novel, and past attempts to translate such a concept into reality have met with success on some occasions and failure on others. The panel believes that a solicitation of proposals emphasizing interactions between academia and the small process technology companies that are capital-poor but problem-rich would prove a worthwhile experiment with a good chance of success.

Report of the
Research Briefing Panel on
Order, Chaos, and Patterns:
Aspects of Nonlinearity

Research Briefing Panel on Order, Chaos, and Patterns: Aspects of Nonlinearity

Mitchell J. Feigenbaum (*Co-Chairman*), Professor of Physics, Rockefeller University

Martin Kruskal (*Co-Chairman*), Professor of Mathematics, Princeton University

William A. Brock, Professor of Economics, University of Wisconsin, Madison

David Campbell, Director, Center for Nonlinear Studies, Los Alamos National Laboratory

James Glimm, Professor of Mathematics, Courant Institute of Science, New York, N.Y.

Leo P. Kadanoff, Professor of Physics, University of Chicago

Anatole Katok, Professor of Mathematics, California Institute of Technology

Albert Libchaber, Professor of Physics, University of Chicago

Arnold Mandell, Director, Laboratory for Biological Dynamics and Theoretical Medicine, University of California, San Diego

Alan C. Newell, Professor of Mathematics, University of Arizona, Tucson

Steven Orszag, Professor of Applied and Computational Mathematics, Princeton University

H. Eugene Stanley, Professor of Physics, Boston University

James Yorke, Acting Director, Institute for Physical Science and Technology, University of Maryland, College Park

Staff

Donald C. Shapero, *Staff Director*

Robert L. Riemer, *Program Officer*, Board on Physics and Astronomy, Commission on Physical Sciences, Mathematics, and Resources

Allan R. Hoffman, *Executive Director*, Committee on Science, Engineering, and Public Policy

Report of the
Research Briefing Panel on
Order, Chaos, and Patterns:
Aspects of Nonlinearity

INTRODUCTION AND BACKGROUND

Linear analysis developed as a formal mathematical discipline during the nineteenth century, and in the intervening years its applications have achieved many spectacular successes throughout science and engineering. But in fact most phenomena observed in nature are nonlinear, and the linear approximations historically used to describe them are too often tacit admissions that the true problems simply cannot be solved. In some instances, including many of technological importance, the effects of nonlinearity can be understood in terms of small perturbations on linear behavior. In other cases, however, incorporation of the true nonlinearities completely changes the qualitative nature of the system's possible behavior. This report focuses on several aspects of these essentially nonlinear phenomena.

The difficulties posed by essential nonlinearity can be illustrated by a familiar example. When water flows through a pipe at low velocity, its motion is laminar and is characteristic of linear behavior: regular, predictable, and describable in simple mathematical terms. However, when the velocity exceeds

a critical value, the motion becomes turbulent, with eddies moving in a complicated, irregular, erratic way that typifies nonlinear behavior. Many other nonlinear phenomena exhibit sharp and unstable boundaries, erratic or chaotic motion, and dramatic responses to very small influences. Such properties typically defy full analytical treatment and make even quantitative numerical description a daunting task. And yet, this task must be confronted, for the point where phenomena become nonlinear is often precisely where they become of interest to technology. In applications ranging from laser/plasma interactions in inertial-confinement thermonuclear fusion, to designs for high-performance and fuel-efficient aircraft, to advanced oil recovery, nonlinearity prevails.

Within the past two decades, the systematic, coordinated investigation of nonlinear natural phenomena and their mathematical models has emerged as a powerful and exciting interdisciplinary subject. Studies of nonlinearity seek to understand a variety of complicated, nonlinear problems encountered in nature and to discover their common features. The scientific methodology has depended on the synergetic blending of three distinct approaches:

- "Experimental mathematics," which is the use of cleverly conceived computer-based numerical simulations, typically involving visualization techniques such as interactive, high-quality graphics, to give qualitative insights into and to stimulate conjectures about analytically intractable problems;

- Novel and powerful analytical mathematical methods to solve, for example, certain nonlinear partial differential equations and to analyze nonlinear stability; and

- Experimental observation of similar behavior in natural nonlinear phenomena in many different contexts and the quantification of this similarity by high-precision experiments.

The success of this three-pronged attack is clearly evidenced by the remarkable progress already made toward solving many nonlinear problems long considered intractable. Essential to this progress has been the discovery that distinct nonlinear phenomena from many fields do indeed display common features and yield to common methods of analysis. This commonality has allowed the rapid transfer of progress in one discipline to other fields and confirms the inherently interdisciplinary nature of the subject. Despite these stimulating developments, however, the present-day approach to nonlinear problems is not entirely systematic. Rather it relies on the identification and exploitation of paradigms, namely, unifying concepts and associated methodologies that are broadly applicable in many different fields.

This report focuses on three of the central paradigms of nonlinearity: coherent structures, chaos, and complex configurations and pattern selection. The following sections cover recent progress in research and future opportunities for research and technological applications of these paradigms, the international standing of U.S. work in the field, and administrative strategies for enhancing progress in this important interdisciplinary subject.

PARADIGMS OF NONLINEARITY: DEFINITIONS, OPPORTUNITIES, AND APPLICATIONS

COHERENT STRUCTURES AND ORDER

From the Red Spot of Jupiter, to clumps of electromagnetic radiation in turbulent plasmas, to microstructures on the atomic scale, long-lived, spatially localized, collective excitations abound in nonlinear systems. These coherent structures show a surprising order in the midst of complex nonlinear behavior and often represent the natural modes for expressing the dynamics. Thus, for example, isolated coherent structures may dominate long-time behavior, and analysis of their interactions may explain the major aspects of the dynamical evolution. Recognition of these possibilities constitutes a fundamental change in the approach to nonlinear systems and has opened up a range of new analytical and computational techniques that yield deep insights into nonlinear natural phenomena.

Although the importance of vortices and eddies in turbulent fluid flows has been appreciated since ancient times, the critical event in the modern concept of coherent structures was the discovery in 1965 of the remarkable "soliton" behavior of localized nonlinear waves governed by the Korteweg–deVries equation, which describes waves in a shallow, narrow channel of water (e.g., a canal) and in many other physical media. Solitons represent coherent structures in the purest sense in that their form is exactly restored after temporary distortion during interactions. Surprisingly, many equations, of wide applicability, have turned out to support solitons, and a major mathematical success has been the revelation that most of these equations can be solved explicitly and systematically by a novel analytical technique known as the inverse spectral transform.

These developments have drawn upon and greatly stimulated several branches of pure mathematics, including infinite-dimensional analysis, algebraic geometry, partial differential equations, and dynamic systems theory. For instance, soliton equations have been shown to correspond to a very special subclass of those nonlinear dynamic systems that have an infinite number of independent parts. Technically, the number of parts is referred to as the number of degrees of freedom or the phase-space dimension. The special characteristic of a soliton equation is that it describes a Hamiltonian dynamic system of infinite phase-space dimension that is, in technical parlance, completely integrable. The Hamiltonian consequently possesses infinitely many independent conservation laws, which determine its behavior. The existence of individual solitons can be understood as a delicate balance between nonlinear focusing and dispersive broadening, while the invariance of solitons under interactions is a consequence of the many conservation laws.

A wide variety of soliton equations has been discovered, allowing a broad range of applications to natural phenomena. In fiber optics, Josephson transmission lines, conducting polymers and other chainlike solids, and plasma ''cavitons,'' the prevailing mathematical models are slight modifications of soliton equations. Thus, with systematic approximations, the behavior of real physical systems can be described quite accurately. An example of potential technological significance can be drawn from nonlinear optics. In this discipline, as the name suggests, nonlinear phenomena, including self-induced transparency, optical phase conjugation, and optical bistability, are dominant. Considerable recent research has investigated the prospect of using solitons to improve long-distance communications in optical fibers. At low intensities, light pulses in optical fibers propagate linearly and tend to disperse, degrading the signal. To compensate for this and reconstruct the pulse, repeaters must be added to the fiber at regular intervals. If the light intensity is increased

into the nonlinear regime, soliton pulses can be formed, the nonlinearity compensating for dispersion. In the idealized limit of no dissipative energy loss, the solitons propagate without degradation of shape; they are indeed the natural, stable, localized modes for propagation in the fiber. Further, realistic theoretical estimates suggest that a soliton-based system could have an information rate one order of magnitude greater than that of conventional linear systems. Although detailed questions of practical implementation remain (primarily costs), the prospects for using optical solitons in long-distance communication are real.

In the more general case, coherent structures interact strongly and do not necessarily maintain their form or even their separate identities for all times. Instabilities generating fluid vortices can lead to vortex pairs, and a pair may merge to form a single coherent structure equivalent to a new and larger vortex. Interactions among shock waves give rise to diffraction patterns of incident, reflected, and transmitted waves. Bubbles and droplets interact through merging and splitting. Significantly, physical examples of these more general coherent structures are nearly universal and, apart from the structures already mentioned, include elastoplastic waves and shear bands, chemical-reaction waves and nonlinear diffusion fronts, phase boundaries, and dislocations in metals. There is a deep mathematical basis to this universality. In a first approximation, these nonlinear wavelike phenomena are subject to conservation laws. In contrast to the soliton case, there are usually only a few conserved quantities (e.g., mass, energy, and momentum). Nonetheless, these few conservation laws strongly restrict the possible behavior of the system. Nonlinearity implies that the speed of a wave depends on the amplitude of the wave itself. As a result, the conservation laws lead to focusing and defocusing of waves. The defocused waves disperse, while the focused waves become coherent structures, the nonlinear modes in which the dynamics is naturally described. They may dominate the long-time behavior of the system, engage in complicated motions and interactions, or organize into complex configurations and patterns.

Fluid vortices—a classic example of which is provided by the Red Spot of Jupiter (Figure 1)—can be used to illustrate the essential role of general coherent structures in nonlinear systems. The existence and stability of the Red Spot of Jupiter have been confirmed since the seventeenth century. A more modern example is the vortex pattern formed in the wake of an airfoil. These vortices are of sufficient size and importance that they govern the allowed spacing between aircraft at landing and thus limit the efficiency of air-port utilization. Similarly, the manner in which vortices are shed from the airfoil strongly affects fuel efficiency and is essential in designing high-performance aircraft. Specifically, vortices are microstructures that make up the critical turbulent boundary layer at the wing surface. More generally, an understanding of the highly nonlinear dynamics of vortices is one of the central problems of applied fluid dynamics.

Further examples of dominant coherent structures can be drawn from almost any field of the natural sciences or engineering. Chemical-reaction fronts are important in many situations and, in flame fronts and internal combustion engines, are coupled strongly to fluid modes. Concentration

Figure 1 A close-up of the giant Red Spot of Jupiter, a coherent structure that exists in the turbulent shear flow in the Southern Hemisphere. Note the coexistence of this large vortex with smaller eddies on many different scales. Although it is not apparent from this single image, the series of time-lapse photographs taken by the Voyager spacecraft shows that the Red Spot is highly dynamic, spinning rapidly and moving westwardly at 11 km/hr. (Courtesy National Aeronautics and Space Administration, Jet Propulsion Laboratory)

fronts arise in the leaching of minerals from ore beds. Fronts between infected and uninfected individuals can be identified in the epidemiology of diseases such as rabies. In geology, elastoplastic waves are important in the slow, long-time deformation of structures. For example, salt domes are formed by a gravitational instability in which the flow of rock layers occurs on geological time scales. Understanding the development of such geological formations is important both theoretically and in the evaluation of potential oil reservoirs. Finally, at the microscopic level the nonlinear dynamics of dislocations may lead to novel effects crucial for interpreting the behavior of materials subjected to high strain rates, and transport phenomena in certain classes of quasi-one-dimensional materials may be controlled by the nonlinear coherent structures they support.

A final example with potential major technological implications is the recent identification of new types of coherent structures and interactions in wave phenomena in oil reservoirs. The essential discovery is that when the speeds of two families of nonlinear waves coincide, a type of nonlinear resonance may give rise to a surprising range of novel wave phenomena. It has recently been shown that nonlinear resonance of this type must occur in three-phase flow in oil reservoirs, and a systematic program is well under way to identify and classify all possible types of nonlinear wave interaction and to assess their importance for oil recovery methods.

Given the ubiquity and importance of coherent structures in nonlinear phenomena, it is gratifying that recent years have witnessed remarkable progress in studying them and that there is great promise for still deeper insights. Significantly, this progress has been achieved by precisely the synergy among computation, theory, and experiment that characterizes nonlinear science. In particular, experimental mathematics has been essential to the understanding of coherent structures and their interactions.

Typically, the forms of the coherent structures are not immediately obvious from the underlying nonlinear equations. Hence visualizations of flow patterns and dynamics using interactive graphics will play an increasingly important role.

In summary, coherent structures reflect an essential paradigm of nonlinear science, providing a unifying concept and an associated methodology at the theoretical, computational, and experimental levels. Their importance for technological applications, as well as their inherent interest for fundamental science, guarantees their central role in all future research in this subject.

CHAOS

The appearance of irregular, aperiodic, intricately detailed, unpredictable motion in deterministic systems is a truly nonlinear effect. Loosely termed chaos, it is remote from linear phenomena. Although chaotic motion is observed, the processes are strictly deterministic: sufficiently accurate knowledge of an initial state allows arbitrarily accurate predictions—but only over a limited interval of time. In particular, it is not necessary to drive a process randomly to observe motion of a stochastic character. Indeed, attempting to model "deterministically chaotic" systems as responding to random forces fails to capture their true behavior.

While the mathematical seeds had already been planted by Poincaré at the turn of the century, they have germinated only in the past three decades, with the advances in interactive computation that we have termed experimental mathematics playing an essential role. One striking recent development has been the recognition that certain chaotic motions unfold themselves with a total lack of regard for the specific mechanisms at work: objects exhibiting certain complex motions follow similar destinies independent of whether their microscopic behavior is governed by equations derived from the theory of chemical interactions, or fluids, or electromagnetism. The discovery of this universality and its application to experiments on the transition to turbulence is one of the triumphs of nonlinear science.

The field of chaotic dynamics continues to undergo explosive growth, with many advances and applications being made across a broad spectrum of disciplines, including physics, chemistry, engineering, fluid mechanics, ecology, and economics. Chaotic systems can be observed in both experimental data and numerical models. Examples include the weather, chemical systems, and beating chicken hearts. The dripping of household faucets can be chaotically irregular, while it has been argued that the satellite Hyperion of Saturn tumbles chaotically in its eccentric elliptical orbit, having no fixed axis because it is constantly kicked by the varying tidal pulls of Saturn.

Medical research has revealed that many physiological parameters vary chaotically in the healthy individual, while more regularity can be a sign of pathology. For example, the familiar pattern of the beating heart is subtly irregular under close examination, and the absence of chaotic components seems to occur in pathological conditions. Similarly, the normally chaotic oscillations of red and white blood cell densities become periodic in some leukemias and anemias. There are many similar examples including periodic catatonias and manic-depressive disorders.

Recent research suggests possible applications to realistic economic models. General equilibrium-theory models have been constructed that are chaotic, but with parameter values that do not mesh well enough with empirical studies to be persuasive. On the other hand economists, motivated by the ideas of chaotic dynamics, have developed new and powerful statistical tests for analyzing time series, which may be useful in other areas of nonlinear science.

As this brief listing suggests, deterministic chaos is essential to the understanding of many real-world nonlinear phenomena. To indicate further aspects of our present understanding, more technical detail is necessary. The concept of the phase-space dimension of a dynamic system was discussed earlier. For a complex object, this dimension is a priori quite high; for a continuous system, such as a fluid, it is in fact infinite. However, if many parts are effectively locked together, as in a coherent structure like a fluid vortex, the effective dimension is reduced, perhaps drastically. This general phenomenon is referred to as mode reduction. As the character of the system's motion changes, so will the number of reduced modes and hence the effective dimension. In the example of pipe flow quoted in the introduction, as velocity increases, the fluid motion becomes suddenly more complex. Such sudden transitions to qualitatively new motions are related to the mathematical phenomenon of bifurcations. Recent advances in the study of bifurcations provide an understanding of the mechanism leading from ordered to chaotic behavior. More specifically, transitions in the behavior of physical systems can arise through an infinite cascade of bifurcations, the best known and first isolated of which is period doubling. This period-doubling cascade is controlled by a special behavior (with certain scaling properties) just at the point of transition, which fully organizes both the orderliness prior to transition and the chaotic behavior after it. Significantly, theory shows that this behavior is correctly expressed by a very low-dimensional, mode-reduced dynamics, independent of the original phase-space dimension of the system. Even more important, the behavior is universal: whatever the system, the properties exhibited are identical. Recent experimental confirmation of these theoretical predictions in systems from convecting fluids to nonlinear electronic circuits is one of the triumphs of nonlinear science.

Once it is recognized that the original equations contain superfluous information because of mode reduction, it becomes important to deduce the actual number of effective equations—that is, the dimension of the reduced system—and then to determine the form of the equations. The first part of this program has been well implemented in the last few years by so-called phase-space reconstruction techniques. Provided that the data support a dimension of below, say, 10, that number can be extracted reliably. Indeed, ideas from thermodynamics provide a graphic depiction that can quickly illuminate some details of the nature of the excitations as well as the dimension. These methods, however, must be refined.

The second part of this program has rarely been accomplished and then only on a case-by-case basis. In some instances, assumed forms can be fit to the data. At this point an easily simulated simple set of equations completely replaces the original ones. For example, three first-order ordinary differential equations exactly replace the full fluid equations throughout a certain regime of motion. Now a real payoff accrues: the model system can easily be time-dependently forced, in contrast to an actual experimental fluid with its physically imposed exigencies, such as boundaries. This can lead to insights of profound technological importance. A recent Soviet effort has apparently succeeded by just this program in forestalling the onset of turbulence in a nozzle flow by imposing periodic stress; clearly such suppression (or enhancement) of turbulence could have many vital applications. More generally, away from transition regions, the specific forms of the mode-reduced equations may play a role. In this regard, an important and generally open problem is to establish the relation, if any, between coherent structures observed in a given motion and the reduced modes that in principle characterize the motion. In certain specific problems, notably perturbed soliton equations and models for chemical-diffusion fronts, progress has been made, but much further research is required.

To delve still deeper into current progress and to indicate what may lie ahead, it is necessary to introduce some additional terminology. For dissipative systems (e.g., those with friction) a wide class of initial motions may in the long-time limit approach some set of phase-space points, which is then called an attractor. Very commonly an attractor is a single point or a closed curve. However, sometimes the attracting set is much more irregular, and for a "strange attractor" the dimension need not even be an integer. This concept of fractional dimension, related to mathematical work begun in the 1920s, has recently become more widely appreciated through the development and application of the theory of such "fractal" objects. Knowledge of fractals is essential to understanding modern nonlinear dynamic systems theory. For example, in a deterministically chaotic system, the attracting set can be a chaotic strange attractor, on which two initially very close points begin to separate exponentially fast. This yields an exquisite sensitivity to initial conditions, for tiny initial uncertainties later produce profound ones. In general, a complicated physical system may contain several attractors, each with its own basin of attraction. A subtle further consequence of nonlinear dynamics is that the boundaries between these basins of attraction can themselves be extraordinarily complex and, in fact, fractal. These fractal basin boundaries mean that totally different long-time behavior can result from indistinguishably close initial configurations.

An illustration of these concepts is provided by weather forecasting. A chaotic dynamic model, based on a crude approximation of atmospheric fluid flow, explains why weather prediction works only for short periods of time. Since small uncertainties grow so rapidly, there is a limit on how far ahead one can predict whether it will rain on a given day, no matter how large and fast the computer that is used to forecast. At the same time, specific familiar local weather patterns—for example, summer thundershowers in the mountains—can be understood in terms of attractors in local models of weather.

Figure 2 depicts a strange attractor found in a model simulation of the behavior of an optical switch. The sequence shown reveals the persistence of the attractor's convoluted structure at successively greater magnifications. This nontrivial structure appearing on all scales correctly suggests that the object does not fill the two-dimensional surface on which it lies, but rather is a fractal with dimension between 1 (a smooth curve) and 2 (a smooth surface). In fact it has dimension 1.7. An unmistakable property of the sequence of Figure 2 is that the very small details are reminiscent of the entire object. This property is called scaling, the formal theory of which allows the construction of fine detail from crude features. Thus, a conceptually new means of describing complicated objects has emerged from these studies. The systematic classification of the strange sets that arise in low-dimensional chaotic motions remains one of the challenges of current studies in nonlinear dynamics.

The impact of deterministic chaos is only now beginning to be felt throughout science. The recognition that even simple systems can exhibit incredibly complicated behavior and that this behavior can be quantified is now widely appreciated and is being applied in many fields. Given the generality of mode reduction and the universality of certain aspects of chaos, the scientific applicability of the concepts of chaotic motion will grow significantly with each step in unraveling these matters.

Complex Configurations and Pattern Selection

When an extended nonlinear system is driven far from equilibrium, the many localized coherent structures that typically appear in it can organize into an enormous range of spatial patterns, regular or random. This process is familiar in turbulent fluid flows (note the complex pattern surrounding the Red Spot in Figure 1) in which temporal behavior is chaotic, but it also occurs in many other phenomena, ranging from mesoscale textures in metallurgy to markings on seashells. The resulting problem of complex configurations and pattern selection represents a third paradigm of nonlinearity.

At present, this paradigm is being investi-

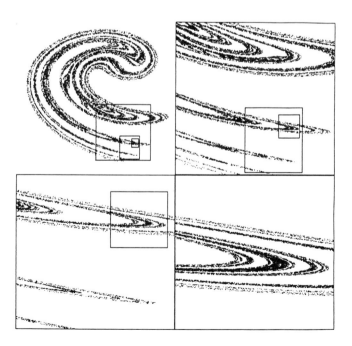

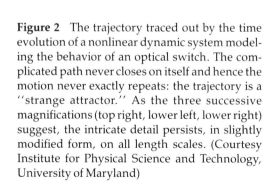

Figure 2 The trajectory traced out by the time evolution of a nonlinear dynamic system modeling the behavior of an optical switch. The complicated path never closes on itself and hence the motion never exactly repeats: the trajectory is a ''strange attractor.'' As the three successive magnifications (top right, lower left, lower right) suggest, the intricate detail persists, in slightly modified form, on all length scales. (Courtesy Institute for Physical Science and Technology, University of Maryland)

48

gated on two levels. The first level is the experimental-mathematical search for complicated, anisotropic configurations that go beyond the highly symmetric patterns that have been accessible via traditional closed form, pencil-and-paper calculations. The second level is the attempt (as in various experimental studies of fluid flows) to determine how they arise dynamically. Nonlinear competitions can determine which particular pattern emerges from the bewildering array typically explored by the chaotic interaction of the individual components.

An increasingly tractable instance of pattern selection is provided by the behavior of unstable fluid interfaces, where instabilities can give rise to entrainment and to a chaotic mixing layer. There are many examples of this phenomenon. An interface separating fluids moving at different velocities is subject to shear instabilities and, through a process

known as roll-up, leads to wound-up vortices along the surface. The original boundary becomes fully entangled by coherent structures (vortices) in the final state. Figure 3 illustrates the complex patterns formed by this shear instability in a case of particular technological importance that was mentioned earlier, namely, the vortices that occur in the wake of an aircraft. Recently, multiple-scale analytic techniques have been applied to derive approximate phase and amplitude equations which, in some fairly simple circumstances, can describe the evolution of these patterns. Another important instance of interfacial instability, with potential technological implications for metallurgical processes and crystal growth problems, occurs in phase transitions in supersaturated or metastable media. Here nonuniform growth of the stable phase produces fingers, known as dendrites, which compete, grow irregu-

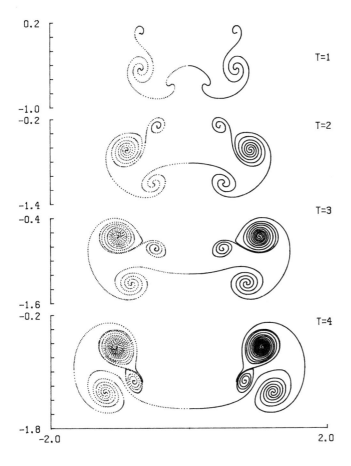

Figure 3 Results of a numerical simulation of vortex sheet model for the shear layer that forms in an aircraft wake. The aircraft is flying perpendicular to and into the plane of the figure. The wake is shown at four positions downstream from the wing's trailing edge. Computational points are drawn on the left, and an interpolating curve is drawn on the right. Initially, the vortex sheet is the straight line segment $-1 \le x \le 1$, $y = 0$, corresponding to the wing's trailing edge. Single-branched wingtip vortices form at the sheet's end points. Double-branched spirals form further inboard due to the effects of deployed flaps and the fuselage. The vortices' roll-up and interaction are strongly nonlinear. (Courtesy Robert Krasny, Courant Institute, "Computation of Vortex Sheet Roll-up in the Trefftz Plane," *Journal of Fluid Mechanics*, in press)

larly, and produce still more complex configurations and patterns, such as found in snowflakes.

To illustrate this interfacial instability in a technologically vital context, we note that the displacement of oil by water in an oil reservoir sometimes leads to an unstable interface. This Saffman–Taylor instability and the resulting viscous fingering are critical to efficient oil recovery; consequently geologists, petroleum engineers, theoretical physicists, applied mathematicians, computer scientists, and experts from other disciplines have focused intensely on this problem. The specific technical issue is that almost half of the oil deposited in limestone or other porous media is typically unrecovered during ordinary oil extraction because it remains stuck in the pores. To recover this oil, a technique called water flooding is used, in which water is injected into the field to force out the oil. The viscous fingering phenomenon often means that nothing is recovered but the injected water, slightly polluted by traces of oil. Clearly a full understanding of this effect and ways to control it are of great importance.

Recent work of a combined experimental, theoretical, and computational nature has led to a semiquantitative understanding of several specific aspects of this problem. First, laboratory experiments have established, under controlled conditions, the nature of the complex configurations that arise in certain parameter ranges of viscous fingering. Figure 4 shows an image of one such configuration in a flat, effectively two-dimensional cylindrical cell. This branched, complex configuration is a fractal. To estimate the fractal dimension, imagine covering the image of the viscous fingering with square cells of side l and calculating, for a given l, the number of cells required to cover the object entirely. As the length of the side l goes to zero, the number of cells required grows as $1/l^d$, where d is the fractal dimension. Performing this calulation for the viscous finger in Figure 3 gives $d = 1.70 \pm 0.05$.

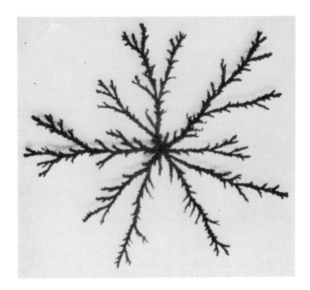

Figure 4 A viscous fingering effect observed when water (black) is forced through a circular inlet in the center of a flat, cylindrical Hele Shaw cell originally filled with high-viscosity fluid. The pattern has a reproducible numerical value, measured by several methods, including the one described in the text, for the fractal dimension of 1.70 ± 0.05. (Courtesy G. Daccord, J. Nittmann, and H. E. Stanley, *Physical Review Letters*, 56:336, 1986)

Hence, this object possesses a fractional dimension closer to that of a plane surface ($d = 2$) than to that of a straight line ($d = 1$). Second, in both the viscous fingering and dendritic growth problems, analytic studies identified an intriguing nonuniqueness to certain features of the pattern selection in the simplest models. Additional physical effects, such as the inclusion of surface tension, were then shown to remove at least in part this nonuniqueness. Although the resulting pattern selection problem has not yet been fully solved, exciting recent progress includes an analytic treatment of effects beyond all orders in perturbation theory. Third, computational simulations have suggested a number of different models and approaches to the problem. Much further research is required, but an accurate and practical procedure for modeling realistic problems now seems possible.

Fractals play an essential role in several

other areas of practical application of the paradigm of complex configurations. In an effort to make ceramics tougher—that is, able to contain a few large flaws without failing—much interest has focused on fractal crack patterns. These arise primarily from two sources: the voids that develop during the sintering process, and the materials harder than ceramics—for example, diamond—normally used to machine them. Instead of moving straight along the surface of the ceramic in a planar path, the propagating crack takes a more tortuous route if it interacts with some microscopic feature of the ceramic—for instance, a second material added to the primary constituent to enhance its toughness. Since the crack will expend more energy in moving out of the plane than it would in propagating unimpeded, it will do less damage to the overall ceramic. Interestingly, the fractal dimension of the crack appears to be related to the fracture toughness of the ceramic. Electron micrographs of cracks put into silica-nitride ceramics, one of the new high-performance materials being considered for high-temperature, high-stress applications such as engine parts, were used to determine the fractal dimension of the cracks. The higher the fractal dimension, the tougher the ceramic.

In certain surface processes, such as roughening, fractal patterns also are observed. For these surface fractals, the lower limit of the fractal dimension is 2, characteristic of a perfectly smooth surface, and the upper limit is 3, a surface so rough and convoluted that it has become a three-dimensional object. The complex configuration of these fractal surfaces can be very important, particularly for processes such as chemical catalysis, where in many cases the higher the fractal dimension of the surface, the greater the catalytic effect.

Many further interesting and relevant illustrations of complex configurations and patterns can be found in nonlinear phenomena from virtually all disciplines. In the biological sphere, the richness of pattern forma-

tion is particularly evident, from tigers' stripes to human digits. Certain features of the problem of morphogenesis can already be understood from plausible nonlinear mathematical models. The development of convection rolls during the transition to turbulence in a fluid heated from below has been extensively studied experimentally and successfully modeled using a combination of computational and analytic techniques. On the other hand, understanding the pattern formation seen in fully developed, three-dimensional turbulence remains one of the most challenging problems of modern science.

Finally, a fascinating class of discrete nonlinear dynamic systems, known as cellular automata, exhibit remarkable pattern formation properties and are currently being subjected to rigorous mathematical scrutiny. At a more speculative level, these highly discrete systems have suggested novel computational algorithms—often called lattice-gas models—for solving certain continuum nonlinear partial differential equations. These algorithms may prove especially valuable for computers based on massively parallel architectures, although both their virtues and their limitations require further study.

This section has focused only on those paradigms of nonlinear science that have been most thoroughly developed and explored, but there are clear indications of many other emerging paradigms. Two are particularly exciting. The concept of adaptation refers to nonlinear dynamic systems that adapt or evolve in response to changes in their environment. Here one crucial aspect is that the nonlinear equations describing the system can themselves be modified on a slow time scale. Among the initial tentative applications of this concept are models for the human immune system and for autocatalytic networks of proteins. A related but somewhat distinct concept is often termed connectionism and reflects the appealing idea that many simple structures connected together can exhibit complex behavior collectively because of the connections. Recent specific instances of this approach include mathematical models called neural networks. Typically only loosely patterned after true neurological systems, these models are remarkable in their promise for being able to learn behavior from experience. The concepts of familiar dynamic systems—such as basins of attraction and coexistence of multiple stable patterns—have already played a crucial role in interpreting the behavior of these more complex systems.

ISSUES, RECOMMENDATIONS, AND CONCLUSIONS

INTERNATIONAL STANDING OF U.S. WORK

Researchers in the United States have played a significant but not dominant role in the recent achievements of nonlinear science. In particular, they have made uniquely important contributions to the experimental mathematics aspect and also provided substantial insights into the experimental and analytic aspects. Nonetheless, the reception of this work within the U.S. scientific community has not been comparable to that seen elsewhere, especially in the Soviet Union and France. In both those countries long-standing traditions in mathematical physics and applied mathematics have helped to stimulate interest in nonlinear phenomena, and the high level of importance that many leading scientists attach to this enterprise is readily noticed in their public comments and in their contributions to the field, particularly in the analytic and experimental areas. Since connections with the active French groups are fairly well established, special emphasis should be placed on strengthening ties with the Soviet efforts, for the United States stands to gain considerably from increased interaction with Russian researchers in this area. From the Soviet perspective, the U.S. leadership in experimental mathematics provides a natural quid pro quo.

In many other countries, work of the highest caliber has been accomplished, and in some there has already been an institutional response, with centers focusing on nonlinear problems established at several universities. It is worth noting that the European Science Foundation recently hosted a meeting on nonlinear science at which the creation of a major European institute on the subject was discussed.

In summary, U.S. research in nonlinear science is of high quality and is widely recognized internationally. Ironically, recognition of this subject within the American scientific community is less developed. Indeed, the interdisciplinary character of the field appears to be problematic for U.S. institutions and agencies. In particular, typical U.S. universities, having departmental structures fairly rigidly defined along traditional disciplines, appear to lack the flexibility to respond adequately to this subject. Students, while interested, seem worried (for good reason) about future positions. In general, while there is strong individual motivation, one hardly senses a more communal national one.

PERSONNEL

Given the interdisciplinary character of nonlinear science, we expect that most of the successful long-term research efforts in this subject will typically result from experts in widely different fields pooling their intellectual resources. Accordingly, agencies and academic administrators should consider both the support of loosely coordinated research networks and the creation of more focused centers in this area. At the same time, however, since many outstanding contributions can be traced to scientists working essentially alone, it is vital to foster and reward high-quality individual research. In particular, the needs of younger scientists eager to become involved but anxious about the lack of a disciplinary base must be confronted. Increased support for junior faculty, postdoctoral fellows, and advanced predoctoral students working on nonlinear problems from an interdisciplinary perspective is clearly necessary. But it is also necessary to ensure the continued input of experts from the traditional disciplines so that studies of nonlinear phenomena address significant and relevant problems.

Several changes in standard university curricula should be contemplated to bring the excitement of this field to still younger students and to train a cadre of potential researchers. With closed-form analyses of interesting nonlinear phenomena infrequent and inadequate, an increased comprehension of the schemes of analysis and calculation is required and the general level of mathematical and computer literacy of all natural-science students should be raised. Coursework in differential equations should include more modern dynamic-systems ideas; calculus should more regularly be followed by deeper courses in analysis; mechanics courses should stress the limitations of perturbation theory and the omnipresence of nonintegrability. A course in numerical methods that leads to intuitive algorithm development based on deep understanding could prepare a researcher to perform meaningful experimental mathematics. Greater exposure should be given to topics such as modern asymptotic and multiple-scale methods, phase and amplitude equations derived from fluids, specific examples of solvable soliton equations, and methods of numerical analysis. Fluids and continuum mechanics should be given higher profiles in physics curricula, and introductory courses in the qualitative phenomenology of chaos and solitons and other nonlinear waves should be generally available. Further, summer institutes focused on specific aspects of nonlinear science should be supported.

FACILITIES

With respect to facilities, one of the major administrative opportunities is the creation of research centers of excellence, either in institutions with preexisting efforts or in response to new proposals. Crucial to this approach is the provision of block or umbrella funding for the interdisciplinary research, rather than balkanization of the research by dividing support among specific disciplines. Again, however, we stress that grants supporting fundamental research by outstanding individuals in this area should be available. These grants should have one or more natural homes within the organizational structures of the federal funding agencies, and special care should be taken that they are not endangered by their interdisciplinary content. On a much grander scale, perhaps one of the proposed National Science Foundation science and technology centers could be devoted to this subject; given its interdisciplinary nature and broad applicability, this may be an attractive prospect.

The central role of computation in nonlinear science clearly suggests that increased access to supercomputers—at the National Science Foundation centers, the National Center for Atmospheric Research, the National Aeronautics and Space Administration, the Department of Energy laboratories, and elsewhere—is vital for continued progress. In particular, interagency cooperation in enhancing supercomputer access is essential. But apart from supercomputer access, individual researchers must be given high-powered scientific work stations with interactive graphics capabilities and a more truly interactive environment. In this matter theorists doing experimental mathematics really do need to be regarded as experimentalists and supported accordingly with the appropriate hardware. Although funding agency awareness of this situation has grown dramatically over the past five years, still greater support is needed.

CONCLUSIONS

As a consequence of its fundamental intellectual appeal and potential technological applications, nonlinear science is currently experiencing a phase of very rapid growth. During this critical period, science administrators in government, education, and industry can play essential roles in further stimulating and guiding this growth. In particular, they can marshal the resources necessary to respond to the challenging research opportunities. In any effort to guide this research, however, it is imperative that nonlinear science be recognized for what it is: an inherently interdisciplinary effort not suited to confinement within any single conventional discipline or department. Hence the administrative structure of research in this area is likely to remain more fragile, and in greater need of attention, than traditional subjects with their natural constituencies. Accompanying this fragility, however, is a remarkable breadth of application and the potential to influence both our basic understanding of the world and our daily life.

Report of the
Research Briefing Panel on
Biological Control
in Managed Ecosystems

Research Briefing Panel on Biological Control in Managed Ecosystems

R. James Cook (*Chairman*), Reseach Leader, Root Disease and Biological Control Research Unit, USDA–ARS–Washington State University, Pullman

Lloyd Andres, Research Entomologist, USDA–ARS, Albany, Calif.

Gustaaf A. de Zoeten, Professor of Plant Pathology, University of Wisconsin, Madison

Charles Doane, Director of Research and Development, Scentry, Inc., Buckeye, Ariz.

Robert W. Gwadz, Scientist Director, USPHS, and Head, Medical Entomology Unit, NAID/NIH, Bethesda, Md.

Ralph W. F. Hardy, President, Boyce Thompson Institute for Plant Research, Ithaca, N.Y.

Bruce Hemming, Research Specialist, Plant Microbiology, Monsanto Life Sciences Research Center, St. Louis, Mo.

Joseph Kuc, Professor of Plant Microbiology, University of Kentucky, Lexington

Reinhold Mankau, Professor of Nematology, University of California, Riverside

David Miller, Staff Scientist, Genetics Institute, Inc., Cambridge, Mass.

Clarence A. Ryan, Jr., Professor of Biochemistry, Institute of Biological Chemistry, Washington State University, Pullman

M. Scott Smith, Associate Professor of Cell Microbiology, University of Kentucky, Lexington

Staff

Clifford J. Gabriel, *Staff Officer,* Board on Basic Biology, Commission on Life Sciences

Allan R. Hoffman, *Executive Director,* Committee on Science, Engineering, and Public Policy

Sandra Anagnostakis, *Consultant,* Connecticut Agricultural Experiment Station, New Haven

Edward Michelson, *Consultant,* Uniformed Services University of the Health Sciences, Bethesda, Md.

George Templeton, *Consultant,* University of Arkansas, Fayetteville

Report of the
Research Briefing Panel on
Biological Control
in Managed Ecosystems

Biological control is the use of natural or modified organisms, genes, or gene products to reduce the effects of undesirable organisms (pests), and to favor desirable organisms such as crops, trees, animals, and beneficial insects and microorganisms. *Managed ecosystems* are environments managed for human benefit. They include farmland, rangeland, forests, lakes, and urban and residential areas. Biological control in managed ecosystems includes the manipulation and strategic introduction of organisms, genes, or gene products to influence the outcome of otherwise natural biological interactions in a manner favorable to humans. Major target pests of biological control are insects, mites, weeds, parasitic nematodes, rodents, and pathogens and their vectors. Achieving successful levels of biological control is dependent on fundamental knowledge of biological interactions at the molecular, cellular, organismal, and ecosystem levels.

Biological control has provided the underpinning of agriculture since ancient times through practices such as crop rotation, intercropping, soil flooding, and tillage. Fortunately, most pests are still suppressed by natural biological controls such as that provided by antagonists (natural enemies) and

self-defense mechanisms (e.g., resistance to pests) that have evolved through long associations between the host plant or animal and its pests. The era of modern biological control began about 100 years ago with the highly successful introduction of the vedalia beetle from Australia into California to control the cottony-cushion scale insect pest of citrus. Nearly 90 years ago, shortly after the rediscovery of Mendel's laws of genetic inheritance, studies of resistance to wheat stem rust provided the first indication that genes for disease resistance in plants could be transferred by conventional breeding.

Because of economic forces and the lack of adequate knowledge about biological controls, many managed ecosystems have become heavily dependent on chemical pesticides. A "spray it" attitude developed, and even today some scientists responsible for research and extension programs tend to think of chemical controls first and of alternative biological controls second. Thus, biological control remains relatively unexplored as an active area of research. In the United States, public and private support for research and development applied to biological control is less than 20 percent of that for chemical control. On a global basis, of the estimated $16 billion spent annually on pest control, less than 1 percent is spent for biological control agents.

WHY BIOLOGICAL CONTROL?

The use of chemical pesticides has produced an increasing number of negative and nontarget effects, and pesticide residues are being found in groundwater and food. Biological controls, however, have resulted in no known or only limited negative effects on the environment. Also, many pests are developing resistance to once-effective pesticides, making it necessary to develop new chemicals or to find effective combinations of chemicals. It is becoming increasingly more difficult and expensive to discover effective chemical pesticides. Although some pests have genetically overcome certain genes for resistance introduced in crop plants, thus far there are no examples of pests becoming resistant to natural enemies, pheromones, or microbial pesticides. Furthermore, many chemicals applied to control pests also destroy beneficial organisms and some create temporary, vacant biological niches that may then provide an opportunity for a new pest or a resurgence of the original one(s). In contrast, biological controls are nearly always targeted for specific pests and are therefore less likely to upset the balance among interacting populations.

Biological control can be achieved by regular or repeated applications of a control agent (e.g., a microbial pesticide) that is specific for a target pest, by a one-time or occasional introduction of a control agent (or genetically resistant crop cultivar) with the ability to establish and keep the target pest in a state of suppression, and by enhancing the effects of indigenous natural enemies (antagonists) of the target pest or maximizing host-plant resistance to the pest through the use of cultural practices (e.g., crop rotation). Some of these biological controls may be initially less effective than many chemical controls, but they are generally more stable and longer lasting. By their nature, biological controls tend to be less dependent than chemical pesticides on fossil energy, and many (e.g., those that achieve control in a single or only occasional application) are self-sustaining.

There are many economically important pests, notably the soilborne pests and insect-vectored pathogens, for which chemical controls are either nonexistent or impractical. Moreover, the modern trend in agriculture toward less or no tillage (for soil conservation) and shorter or no crop rotation has favored increased damage from soilborne pests. Unfortunately, the use of high-energy production inputs such as fertilizer and irrigation are commonly increased to compensate for inadequate pest control or to attain greater crop yields despite the pest damage. Biological control achieved through greater knowledge of ecology and strategic introductions of beneficial organisms or genetic resistance in the crop may offer the only means of stably and effectively controlling these intractable pest problems. Any gain in control over these pests is a gain for production efficiency, since yields are increased without requiring more fertilizer or water. Thus, biological control is not only an alternative to chemical control, it also greatly helps industries such as agriculture conserve resources and become more sustainable and efficient with fewer negative effects on the environment (Table 1).

The development of recombinant DNA technology is unquestionably the most significant advance thus far for biological control research. Recombinant DNA techniques enable scientists to understand the mechanisms of biological control at the molecular level in ways previously not possible. Understanding the genes and gene products important to biological control opens the way for the genetic alteration of the agents carrying these genes, for the production of more useful transgenic biological control agents, and for deriving improved practices to enhance biological control.

TABLE 1 Potential Benefits from Biological Control Research

Farming	Agribusiness Input	Food Processing	Consumer	Society	International
Improved production efficiency leading to a more favorable competitive standing in domestic and export markets	New high-value products for national and international markets	Decreased levels of agrichemical residues in commodities for food	Low-cost food Increased quality (healthfulness) of food	Cleaner, safer environment	Improved competitiveness
Reduced health risk from agrichemicals					
Plant protection for new or modified crops					

COMPONENTS OF BIOLOGICAL CONTROL

The components of biological control (Table 2) can include a pest agent used against itself (e.g., pheromones and sterile males of insect pests), a host plant or animal we seek to protect whose defense mechanisms have been enhanced through management or genetic manipulation, and the pest's natural enemies and antagonists (the classic biological control agents). These components and the approaches to their management provide the basis for three major biological control strategies:

1. *Regulation of the pest population:* biological control agents are used to regulate the pest population at or below an acceptable threshold.

2. *Exclusionary systems of protection:* beneficial microorganisms are used as a living barrier that excludes infection or deters pest attack.

3. *Self-defense:* resistance mechanisms in the plant or animal host itself prevent or suppress disease or pest damage.

All of these strategies can be demonstrated by the multiple uses of the *Bacillus thuringiensis* (Bt) toxin, a protein lethal to certain insects. The bacterium *B. thuringiensis* has long been marketed throughout the world as a highly effective and safe microbial pesticide for use against some insect pests. With the tools of recombinant DNA technology, the Bt toxin gene has now been transferred to, and expressed in, both the common soil bacterium *Pseudomonas fluorescens* and tobacco plants. Therefore, when the toxin gene is expressed in its native *B. thuringiensis*, it can regulate the pest population (Strategy 1). When *B. thuringiensis* is applied as a microbial pesticide on plants or when the toxin gene is expressed in *P. fluorescens*, which grows on corn roots, it protects against insect attack by operating as an exclusionary system on the plant host (Strategy 2). Finally, when the gene is expressed in tobacco leaves, it limits pest damage by functioning as a self-defense system within the plant host (Strategy 3). Undoubtedly the flexibility made possible by recombinant DNA tech-

TABLE 2 Selected Examples of Biological Controls

Component	Strategy		
	Regulation of the Pest Population	Exclusionary Systems of Protection	Self-Defense
Pest agent used against itself	Pheromone gossypol to control pink bollworm in cotton in Egypt, South America, and the United States Sterile males to control screw worm in the United States Mosquitoes genetically incapable of vectoring the malaria agent used to displace capable types[a]	Avirulent strain K-84 of *Agrobacterium* for control of crown gall on fruit trees and ornamental plants in several countries Ice-minus strains of *Pseudomonas syringae* to exclude ice-nucleation-active strains from leaves of frost-sensitive plants[a]	Mild strains of citrus tristeza virus to protect citrus against virulent strains of the virus in Australia and Brazil Resistance to tobacco mosaic virus (TMV) in tobacco plants genetically engineered to express the coat-protein gene of TMV[a]
Natural enemies and antagonists (classic biological control agents)	Wasps for control of the alfalfa weevil in the United States Predatory snail for control of snail vector of schistosomiasis agent in Puerto Rico *Puccinia* rust for control of skeleton weed in Australia and the United States *Bacillus thuringiensis* for control of certain caterpillars—used worldwide	*Phlebia gigantea* applied to pine stumps to exclude the pine root-rot fungus *Heterobasidion annosum* Nonpathogenic *Lactobacillus* strains used to exclude *Escherichia coli* from the intestinal lining and protect piglets against neonatal scours[a] Toxin gene from *B. thuringiensis* expressed in *Pseudomonas* on corn roots for protection against certain soil insects[a]	"Immunization" (induced resistance) of cucumbers and other plant species against *Colletotrichum* (anthracnose) by inoculating their leaves with tobacco necrosis virus[a] Toxin gene from *B. thuringiensis* expressed in tobacco leaves for control of certain leaf-feeding caterpillars[a]
Host plant or animal	*Crotalaria* grown as a trap plant; root-knot nematode infects this plant but does not reproduce—minor use in the United States	Dense sowings of cereal-grain crops to preempt the establishment of weeds—used worldwide	Genetic resistance to southern corn leaf blight in corn in the United States Genetic resistance to Hessian fly in wheat in the United States

[a]Experimental stage only.

nology will provide other new uses for other traditional biological control agents.

For managed ecosystems, integrated multiple biological controls are common and tend to be more effective than single-shot tactics. This may account for the relatively stable nature of biological control. A system is generally developed first by using cultural practices, such as crop rotation and tillage, that maximize the effect of the natural (indigenous) biological controls and then by introducing specific controls, such as certain genes for resistance to pests, exotic enemies of naturalized pests, or inundative applications of biological control agents in cases in which the natural populations are too small to be effective.

SUCCESSFUL BIOLOGICAL CONTROLS

REGULATION OF THE PEST POPULATION (STRATEGY 1)

Many (probably most) pests do not become economically important until they escape their own natural enemies or until other constraints on the pest population are eased. This generally happens when the pest is inadvertently introduced into a new environment. The great majority of economically important pests in the United States, for example, were accidently introduced as a result of commerce. It has been estimated that 11 new insect pests are inadvertently introduced into the United States each year. For some of these pests, successful control has been achieved by tracking down their original source and then finding and introducing one or more of their natural enemies. A classic example of this is the control for the past 50 years of the *Opuntia* cactus in Australia, following the introduction from South America of a moth (*Cactoblastis cactorum*) that feeds on that cactus. In the United States, more than 70 candidate plant-feeding insects and plant pathogens (all fungi) have been introduced to control target weed species. These organisms were first selected because they are specifically adapted to feed on or parasitize the target weeds. About 14 weed species are now partly or completely controlled in the United States in this way. Almost five times this number of naturalized insect pests have been controlled in the United States through the introduction of exotic parasites, predators, or pathogens.

Tracking down the source of the pest can be difficult, especially if its origin is not readily accessible, such as in the People's Republic of China,* the Middle East, or the USSR,

*Henceforth referred to as "China."

all of which are sources of major U.S. pests. Moreover, in testing biological control agents to be used against weeds, the number of plant species that must be examined is increasing because of growing concern that the agent may also attack nontarget plant species. Once released, the biological control agent must be monitored for several years within the ecosystems in which the releases were made as well as within adjacent ecosystems. Thus far, no insect or microorganism introduced for pest control in the United States has itself become a pest.

EXCLUSIONARY SYSTEMS OF PROTECTION (STRATEGY 2)

A method discovered in Australia for biological control of crown gall on ornamental shrubs and orchard trees is based on an exclusionary system that prevents the crown-gall pathogen from infecting the plant. The pathogen population may then decline through attrition, but this is secondary to keeping the plant healthy. Crown gall is caused by *Agrobacterium tumefaciens*, a soil bacterium that infects roots and stems through wounds such as those that occur during transplanting. In the biological control system, an avirulent *Agrobacterium* is used to protect wounds against the virulent *Agrobacterium*. This biological control agent (known as strain K-84) lacks the genetic means to incite gall formation and produces a substance that inhibits the pathogen. Bareroot transplants dipped in a cell suspension of K-84 are protected for most or all of their life.

In another exclusionary type of biological control, which was developed in England, a nonpathogenic fungus is used to protect pines against root rot. This biological control agent and K-84 were the first two agents registered by the Environmental Protection Agency (EPA) for use in the United States against plant diseases. It took 10–15 years to develop each system, both of which are now used in many countries.

Another control aimed at exclusion has the potential for protecting livestock against certain pathogens. A U.S. company has developed a product consisting of live cells of a nonpathogenic *Lactobacillus fermentum*, which occupies attachment sites on the intestinal lining when introduced into newborn piglets. This preempts the attachment to the lining of the strain of *Escherichia coli* responsible for neonatal scours.

SYSTEMS OF SELF-DEFENSE
(STRATEGY 3)

Plants and animals have evolved many effective defense mechanisms that are subject to improvement by conventional breeding and by genetic engineering. For example, the last major epidemic of wheat stem rust in the Great Plains of the United States occurred over 30 years ago; this success is due to the introduction of genes for resistance as necessary according to results of annual surveys for virulence genes in the pathogen population. Although they are not within the scope of this report, vaccines have been the most successful biological control of diseases of humans and livestock. Plants have no immune system comparable to that of animals, but they can be effectively protected against disease agents by inoculation with avirulent strains related to the pathogen or with a microorganism that is pathogenic to another plant. For example, the citrus tristeza virus from Africa was introduced into South America in the 1920s and nearly decimated the citrus industries of Argentina, Brazil, and Uruguay until biological control was developed. In 1951, mild strains of the tristeza virus complex in Brazil were found to protect trees against severe strains. Commercial testing of these strains was begun in 1968, and by 1980, 8 million trees were protected in Brazil by deliberate inoculation of seedlings with a mild strain. The same method is also used in Australia. Thus far, there is no evidence that the control is likely to break down or cause any detrimental nontarget effects.

RECENT ADVANCES IN RESEARCH ON BIOLOGICAL CONTROL

NEW APPROACHES TO THE REGULATION OF PEST POPULATIONS

Scientists are continuing to discover natural enemies of pests and to find better ways to track and favor these beneficial organisms. Microbial pesticides are a particularly promising aspect of this classic approach and are becoming recognized by both established and start-up industries as opportunities for commercial development.

At least four baculoviruses are now registered by the EPA for use as microbial insecticides, but none are commercially available in the United States. Baculoviruses are expensive to mass produce for large-scale distribution and are slow to kill target insects. Special processes are being designed to decrease the cost of production, and attempts to accelerate the kill speed are being made by genetic manipulation of the baculovirus genome (chromosome). For example, a toxin gene can be substituted for or inserted into a nonessential virus gene, so that the toxin is produced on ingestion by the insect and kills it more quickly than the viral infection would.

Microbial herbicides can rapidly and selectively eliminate weeds from managed ecosystems with an effectiveness similar to that of chemical herbicides. Two microbial herbicides are now commercially available in the United States for control of relatively minor weeds. These microbial herbicides are formulations of living, host-specific fungal pathogens, and were discovered around 1970. Their commerical development resulted from the effective collaboration of the public and the private sectors. No hazards to human health or other nontarget effects have been observed for either of these microbial herbicides.

Several genetic traits are known to render

mosquitoes refractory to the transmission of the malaria parasite *Plasmodium falciparum.* In a novel approach to malaria control, it has been proposed that genetic manipulation could be used to transfer genes to mosquitoes rendering them incapable of transmitting the parasite. These mosquitoes would be expected to compete with and replace indigenous vector types. This approach might be extended to vectors of plant viruses, but we must first amass a great deal more fundamental information, including information on vector specificity for pathogen strains, pathogen reservoirs, and the genetics of virulence and transmission.

MANAGEMENT OF BENEFICIAL PLANT-MICROBE ASSOCIATIONS

Plants support large populations of microbes (bacteria and fungi) as indigenous cosmopolitan inhabitants of their leaves, stems, and roots. These microbes may well provide the first level of defense of plants against pests. Some of the more beneficial plant–microbe associations include mycorrhizal fungi that help the plant take in nutrients and water while providing some protection against root disease, fungi within plant tissues (endophytes) that produce substances that inhibit or are obnoxious to insect pests, and microorganisms on the leaves and roots (epiphytes) that compete with and inhibit pathogens even before they enter the plant. These types of potential biological control agents can be applied to seeds or other planting material and therefore represent significant opportunities for commercial development.

Recent studies conducted in Australia, Canada, China, the Netherlands, and the United States reveal the potential of root-colonizing microorganisms to inhibit or displace pathogens at the root–soil interface and thereby protect the root health of perennial and annual plants. These microorganisms inhibit root pathogens by producing antibiotics, siderophores (compounds that

chelate biologically available iron), and possibly substances that stimulate plant growth. One such biological control is the use of bacterial strains of *Pseudomonas fluorescens* and *P. putida* (root-colonizing bacteria) to protect wheat roots against the soilborne fungus *Gaeumannomyces graminis* var. *tritici.* This fungus incites an important disease of wheat called "take-all." Take-all is enhanced by the current trend toward less crop rotation and less tillage and has become the most economically important root disease of wheat worldwide. The benefical bacteria were discovered during basic research on the natural history of a spontaneous decrease in severity of take-all—a natural biological control that sometimes follows two or three outbreaks of the disease and the continued monoculture of wheat. The bacteria thrive on wheat roots infected with *G. graminis* and are believed to provide this natural biological control. The most effective strains produce phenazine-type antibiotics that are strong inhibitors of *G. graminis.* The effective strains tested on crop plants so far occur naturally, but the genes for phenazine production are being isolated and will be available in the future to improve strains by genetic engineering.

ADVANCES THROUGH UNDERSTANDING THE MOLECULAR BIOLOGY OF SELF-DEFENSE

Rapid advances are being made in research on the use of natural defense systems of plants in biological control. Most if not all plants are thought to have the genetic potential to protect themselves from infectious agents and from most insect and nematode pests. Damage results when the pest agent somehow circumvents or suppresses this defense mechanism by its own genetically controlled mechanisms. In addition to genetic improvement of resistance in plants, these defense mechanisms can be induced by inoculating the host plant with avirulent pathogens.

Induced resistance in plants occurs in response to all categories of plant pathogens and to certain insect pests. For example, beans, cucumbers, watermelons, and muskmelons can be systemically protected against diseases caused by fungi, bacteria, or viruses by prior inoculation with agents that are capable of causing only restricted infections. This protection persists for essentially the entire crop season. When certain chewing insects begin to feed on the leaves of potatoes or tomatoes, a systemic signal triggered by small fragments of plant cell-wall material activates genes in distant leaves for synthesis of protease inhibitors. Insects acquire the protease inhibitors while feeding on these leaves. The insects' own digestion, physiology, and growth are then inhibited, and they cease feeding on that plant. This provides an advantage to the plant and the predators that feed on the insect pest. Investigators are now trying to transfer these genes for insect-induced synthesis of protease inhibitors to those plants without them.

Studies of plant virus infection indicate that virus coat protein protects the plant cells against subsequent infection by a closely related strain of the virus—a type of cross-protection. On the basis of these studies, tobacco plants resistant to tobacco mosaic virus (TMV) were produced by recombinant DNA technology. The TMV gene for coat protein was transferred to and expressed in tobacco and tomato plants, resulting in cross-protection without inoculating plants with the protecting virus strain. This method has also been extended to alfalfa mosaic virus control. This approach to virus control is a major advance and avoids any potential risks associated with the use of mild virus strains in the field.

RESEARCH OPPORTUNITIES

The diversity of natural systems provides a wealth of potential biological control agents, including viruses, bacteria, and fungi. Although many collections of these organisms exist, additional research is needed to collect, characterize, and select the most promising agents. In many cases, such as the baculoviruses for insect control, more efficient and less costly production processes need to be developed. Stabilization of biological activity during formulation and delivery is another need for many biological control agents. This complex field will require the integration of biological and engineering skills. Biotechnology is expected to provide a means for developing a more complete understanding of biological interactions and for expanding genetic manipulations of organisms to make biological control practical on a broader scale.

Opportunities for research to develop new or improved methods of biological control are virtually unlimited. For example, mycoviruses (viruses of fungi) are associated with loss of fungal virulence (hypovirulence) in the fungi responsible for chestnut blight and Dutch elm disease. In France, chestnut trees are recovering where virus-infected (less virulent) strains of the chestnut blight fungus were introduced. The introduction of virus-infected strains has not worked in the United States, because "mating" of fungus strains must occur for the virus to be transmitted and there are many incompatible mating groups among the chestnut blight fungi within the country. Nevertheless, research on these viruses and other similar fungal pathogens deserve increased attention.

Opportunities for the biological control of viral diseases will be gained mainly through molecular approaches, such as genetic engineering to introduce resistance genes into plants, inhibiting virus multiplication with antisense viral RNA (viral RNA that is complementary to the messenger-sense RNA), and building on the molecular basis for cross-protection. As knowledge of how viruses infect, multiply, and affect their hosts increases, so does our ability to control viral diseases.

For root diseases, greater study is needed of the pathogen-suppressive soils—those soils with unique microbiological properties that prevent pathogens from becoming established or from causing disease. Such soils have also been reported for certain soil-inhabiting insect pests. Knowledge of the mechanisms of suppression is providing useful new information on the ecology of such pests and is leading to the discovery of new biological control agents.

There are almost unlimited opportunities to be explored in the biological control of nematodes. The pathogenic bacterium *Pasteuria penetrans* is one possible biological control agent for several economically important nematodes, but as for so many other potential biological control agents, there is no economic means to produce it on a large scale. Another, but less efficient biological control of nematodes is the use of plants, such as *Crotalaria spectabilis*, that prevent the nematode from reproducing. These plants might be made to provide more efficient nematode control or could perhaps be used in insect control if they could be genetically engineered to produce attractants or pheromones.

Fundamental to all areas of biological control is basic research on interspecific and intraspecific communications, such as, how insect pests find their host plants, how plants repel insects, how natural enemies find their prey, or how individuals within the mating population of a species find or avoid one another so that the population becomes inbred or genetically more diverse. Information on local and systemic signals transmitted within plants when they are wounded or challenged by a pest will help us understand the mechanisms of recognition and defense that are important to biological control applications. Basic research in population biology, organism–environment interactions, physiological ecology, and other areas is essential to the discovery, conservation, and enhancement of future biological controls.

Solving these problems in basic and applied research in biological control will require the continuation of traditional single-investigator projects; however, problems involving such complex matters as understanding and improving mechanisms of biological control, testing and integrating systems in the field, and tracking specific organisms in the ecosystem can be efficiently solved only by multidisciplinary teams of well-trained scientists. Such teams should include geneticists, biochemists, molecular biologists, microbiologists, physiologists, plant pathologists, entomologists, and ecologists. Mathematicians should work with ecologists in modeling the complex interactions that occur in biological control to help provide a basis for prediction. Economists and sociologists must become involved to help guide projects from the standpoint of feasibility, acceptability, and integration with established practices. The commercialization of biological control products will also require extensive research in mass production, formulation, and delivery of these agents.

WORLD STATUS OF U.S. BIOLOGICAL CONTROL RESEARCH, DEVELOPMENT, AND APPLICATION

CURRENT U.S. POSITION

The United States leads the world in the discovery and reporting of biological phenomena related to biological control. It also ranks first in the development of recombinant DNA and computer technology, both of which are needed to understand and improve systems of biological control. However, except for the conventional breeding of plants with improved resistance and the release of exotic enemies of naturalized pests (classic biological control), the United States in general is not the leader in the use of biological control.

Many nations have indicated or demonstrated a greater commitment to understanding biological control and to making it work. For example, research on biological control of plant viruses is not as extensive in the United States as it is in the Netherlands. The United States is a leader in the biological control of weeds, but Australia, a nation with only a fraction of the U.S. resources, has an effort that is almost as great. The first (and so far only) two biological agents for controlling plant pathogens registered by the EPA for use in the United States came from England and Australia. The Federal Republic of Germany has a greater total effort than the United States in the biological control of plant-parasitic nematodes. The United States is the leader in research on insect pheromones, but large foreign companies are increasing their involvement in this approach to biological control. The United States along with Western Europe and Canada have the strongest programs in basic research on insect pathogens, but Brazil, China, and the USSR have the greatest experience in the use of microbial insecticides.

The United States has also been less successful than many countries in its efforts to assemble interdisciplinary teams of scientists to focus on biological control. China identified biological control as a priority in its seventh 5-year plan and has committed major resources to this area of research since 1979 (the year biological control teams were exchanged between the United States and China). In China, important pest complexes have been targeted for biological control, and teams of researchers are now being assembled to conduct the necessary research. These new Chinese research projects are based on U.S. technology. Belgium has one of the largest interdisciplinary teams for conducting mainly basic but also applied research on plant–microbe associations; few if any existing U.S. groups can compete with teams such as these. Several countries, including Canada and Great Britain, have formalized links between public agencies and private companies as a way to assemble large enough groups to conduct research on the application of biotechnology, including biological control technology.

U.S. PROSPECTS

The United States has many advantages that could make it a world leader in the application and marketing of biological controls while also increasing its contribution of new scientific information basic to the field. It has many repositories of biological material with the raw germplasm to develop superior biological controls, including those with marketable components. The way is now clear in the United States for exclusive licensing of biological control agents by commercial firms, including agents developed in and patented by state or federal laboratories. The United States has an advantage in the composition of its industrial infrastructure, which ranges from cottage industries and start-up companies to leading multinational corporations.

Perhaps the single greatest advantage of the United States relative to other countries is the human resource within its network of academic institutions. No other country can match the U.S. supply of young people highly trained in molecular biology, computer technology, ecology, and other sciences fundamental to future research and development in biological control. However, competition for limited funding is so intense that agencies such as the National Science Foundation, the National Institutes of Health (NIH), and the U.S. Department of Agriculture (USDA) with interests in this area are funding only a small fraction of all proposals. Funding agencies need to direct or encourage a portion of these resources toward fundamental and applied studies in biological control.

Another major U.S. advantage is its Land Grant University and USDA/State Agricultural Experiment Station system. No other experiment station system in the world has the capability or experience in field testing and in developing the management strategies to integrate biological control into agriculture, forestry, and other managed ecosystems. This system can also provide links with user communities through education and demonstrations, and employs economists who can help determine economic feasibility.

NEEDS AND RECOMMENDATIONS

BASIC RESEARCH

Two types of basic research needs can be identified. First is the obvious need for more basic research in areas such as ecology, genetics, physiology, cell biology, and molecular biology to provide adequate knowledge about biological interactions, especially those that can be modified for biological control. The second need is more subtle. It concerns the perceptions among researchers that biological control is a narrow and applied field of study. As a result, many people working in areas fundamental to biological control have generally not thought of their research as potentially relevant to biological control. Practitioners must also adopt a broader concept of biological control than they have in the past.

SOLVING THE COMPLEX PROBLEMS

A major limitation in the United States is the lack of the sustained, concentrated, and interdisciplinary effort needed to solve complex problems in both basic and applied biological control research. Individual investigators have tended to conduct short-term, descriptive research on an interesting biological control phenomenon, publish one or a few papers, and then move on to another research topic. The U.S. scientific literature is replete with isolated reports of biological control, but few of these reports are actually followed-up. Because of the inherent difficulty and long-term nature of the work, investigators lose interest, become discouraged, or stop because their funding is too short term. The United States needs to support multidisciplinary teams that have the potential for sustained research in solving the complex problems related to biological control, while simultaneously continuing to support individual investigators. Such groups could be formed across departmental boundaries within a research or academic institution, between two or more academic institutions, or between public and private organizations. In addition, training grants could be used to attract and support graduate students or postdoctoral associates in the more productive or successful laboratories or as members of a multidisciplinary team working on biological control. Career-development grants, possibly patterned after the NIH model, could be used to help sustain young scientists for 5–10 years so that they could continue their work on specific projects in biological control.

MOVING RESEARCH OUT OF THE LABORATORY

Even under the most efficient circumstances, the transfer of biological control research from the laboratory to the field is a slow process. Researchers in public-supported institutions tend to avoid lengthy field tests that involve several geographic locations because they are expensive and because the chance of obtaining successful results has been low. The private sector, on the other hand, has generally been reluctant to invest in developing products for the narrow, specialized markets typical of so many biological controls. The problems for biological control development are compounded by regulatory issues and questions concerning the guidelines and protocols that must be followed, whether conducting basic research or testing biological control agents in the field. Pharmaceutical products developed through biotechnology are reaching the marketplace much faster than products for biological control, in part because of accelerated regulatory approval by the Food and Drug Administration.

A special grants program available to both public and private researchers could be initi-

ated to support field research. Incentives for the private sector and more cooperative ties between the public and private sectors (e.g., joint ventures) are also needed to accelerate research on product development. Several small companies and three or four of the larger corporations have begun to invest in the development of biological control products in the United States, which shows that interest in commercial development of biological control is growing in the U.S. private sector.

Existing state and federal programs on pilot testing of biological control systems and on obtaining data for registration of minor-use biological control products are important. These programs could play a larger role in the transfer of technology from the laboratory to commercial applications. The development of protocols for field research and testing should take into account the fact that during the 99 years of modern biological control, there are few, if any, examples of a biological control agent (i.e., an insect, pheromone, microbe, or gene) having a known or significant negative effect on the environment after its deliberate introduction. Thus, the existing regulations of the USDA Animal and Plant Health Inspection Service for importation and release of potential pests (or organisms related to pests) seem adequate for regulation of nonengineered biological control agents. In addition, the guidelines developed by the NIH Recombinant DNA Advisory Committee (RAC) for laboratory research with genetically engineered organisms seem to be an appropriate model for the creation of guidelines on the field testing of genetically engineered biological control agents. Regarding final registration, there is no evidence that biological control products developed using recombinant DNA technology will require regulation that is any different from those products developed via nonengineering processes. Regulations should be based on the product's properties and not on the process used to make it. Field research with pheromones and nonengineered, non-

pathogenic microorganisms should require protocols no different from the traditional procedures used for field research on nonengineered nitrogen-fixing bacteria or new plant cultivars.

CONCLUSIONS

Biological control can and should become the primary method used in the United States to ensure the health and productivity of important plant and animal species. The need for alternatives to complement or replace chemical control dictates placing an increasing emphasis on biological control research and development. Chemical pesticides are responsible for a wide array of unacceptable negative environmental effects. For example, they tend to create fluctuating cycles of pests because they lead to selection for resistance in the pest population, and they tend to eliminate beneficial as well as harmful organisms. In contrast, biological controls have had no known or significant negative, nontarget effects; instead, they maintain the biological balance through adjustments in the management of ecosystems and by the strategic introduction of organisms or their genes to influence the outcome of natural biological interactions. Advances in biotechnology greatly facilitate the development of successful new biological controls and the more effective manipulation of natural forms of biological control. Major factors preventing greater use of biological controls include a lack of basic information on ecology and biological interactions, an inadequate interdisciplinary effort to solve complex problems, and constraints on moving research from the laboratory to the field. The development of biological control as the foundation of pest control in the United States is the most important challenge we face in making safe and efficient use of our managed ecosystems.